Sales Drive

The definitive 'no-brainer' street smart guide to Sales Stardom

By
Phil Polson

Published in Australia by the 3 Elements Group.

www.salesdrive.com.au

The 3 Elements Group
G.P.O Box 2867 Sydney,
NSW, 2001
Australia

Fax: +61 2 8456 5708

Printed by: CreateSpace, a DBA of On-Demand Publishing, LLC

Polson, Phil
Sales Drive: The definitive street-smart 'no-brainer' guide to Sales
Stardom

ISBN-13:
978-1468032086

ISBN-10:
1468032089

Dedication:

This book is dedicated to the loving memory of my late cousin.

James Arthur Rose. (1948-2011).

He was a man of the land, a farmer, a hard working, and honest toiler. A favourite cousin of mine, Jim was a loving father, a consummate salesperson, a compassionate listener, good friend, and great storyteller.

He was a big-hearted, true gentleman.

Above all he was a great human being.

Rest in Peace, Big Jim.

Foreword

Early in the text, Phil Polson quotes a Chinese proverb:

> *"The person who says it cannot be done should not interrupt the person who is doing it."*

Many who encounter this unusual book will come into the creative arena carrying an assumption – what Phil has accomplished, as he composed the unique contents, can't be done. Oh, yes, it can ... and you'll see that his bright and valuable information, salted with lighthearted anecdotes, is a masterpiece of communication. Phil combines a hard-boiled analysis of the creative process with his rare sense of humour. Bravo, Phil.

Examples clarify every major point, and never does one sense a pedantic overtone. What a pleasure that is!

On a slightly different plateau: Anyone and everyone involved in the sales process not only should read the chapter on "Different Sales Levels" but read it a second time to be sure of absorption.

Gems galore! Incentive programs that backfire ... incentive programs that are golden ... the clinker hidden in incentives ... you get the idea.

The purpose of a foreword isn't to synopsise a book but to point out reasons for enthusiasm in reading it. So I won't take up space repeating what Phil Polson says better.

Instead, I'll just congratulate you for having the perspicacity to acquire a book that can be a positive cornerstone of your ongoing career. And, oh...

Thanks, Phil, on behalf of all of us, for writing it.

-- Herschell Gordon Lewis

As a communicator in the sophisticated world of direct marketing, Herschell Gordon Lewis is without peer.

Nobody has written more books. Nobody has written more articles.

Certainly nobody is more respected. Herschell is the world's most respected copywriter and he is also a renowned filmmaker.

Contents

About the Author

Phil Polson was born in Christchurch, New Zealand. Both of his parents died within a week of each other when he was young, leaving himself and two older sisters to largely fend for themselves. His loving sisters, many relatives, and kind friends played an integral part in his upbringing.

From a background in the building and construction industry, he built numerous houses for himself in his spare time. In 1981, he co-founded one of the first sales, management, and motivation training companies in Australasia. He was an innovator of the large Public Seminar industry and the Cruise ship seminar concept. The inaugural ship presentation featured among others Robert Waterman co-author of the best selling management book "In Search Of Excellence" on the P & O ocean liner Island Princess also known as televisions "Love Boat' during the America's Cup challenge off Fremantle, WA. Rare spare time on board was taken up learning the card game, bridge. A newspaper clipping appears in the back of the book as evidence of that. This company quickly became amongst the largest facilitators of seminars in the world, promoting many of the biggest names in the industry, (an extended list of which appears in the post face of this book).

The business expanded in Australia in the mid eighties. The original owners gradually went their separate ways in related fields. Phil migrated to Australia in 1997. He has been involved on a consultative basis in management and sales for the construction industry, manufacturers, financial, wealth creation, retail, chemical, pharmaceutical, oil, mining and brewing companies. He has been invited by a number of specialist professionals to become part of a network that offers highly specialised solutions to companies and higher net worth individuals. These solutions encapsulate sales growth, sales audits, joint sales ventures, peak motivation, as well as structuring sustainable executive incentive packages. The critical success of all these solutions are founded on the COG® System which is fully explained throughout the pages of this book

The team knows that no one person has all the knowledge and wisdom necessary for sales and business success at all levels. They understand that collective sharing of wisdom is a far more powerful force. This tight team operates under the 3 Elements Group banner and can be contacted via email at info@3eg.com.au, their website www.salesdrive.com.au, by mail GPO Box 2867 Sydney NSW 2001, or by fax, +61 2 8456 5708.

Phil's hobbies include coaching rugby, swimming, golf, cycling, sailing, and cricket. He also collects classic cars, loves cooking, and cultivates orchids.

The Professional Sales Champions Operational Guide to Selling Stardom! COG®.

Diagram 'A'.

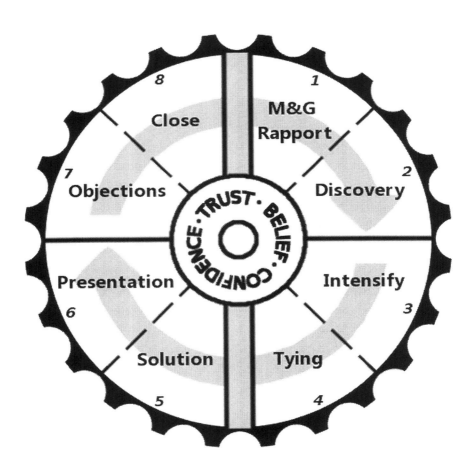

A diagrammatic explanation of "COG": **Diagram 'A'.**

We call the system "COG" for short. COG is a complete set of sales tools that once learned, you can carry in your mind. Once you know the system as described in this book whenever you are in a selling situation you will automatically see the COG in your head. All you have to do is picture the COG, shown in diagram 'A', and you will always know exactly where you are in the selling process. You will then know exactly which tool to take out of your mental 'tool-kit' and use for the right job. Depending on prospects responses and their knowledge and enthusiasm you can either wind the COG back to an earlier stage or go forward if the occasion requires you to speed up a little. For example, if you are in front of a prospect that is at level 101 on the subject of your specialty, product or service. You may need to slow down, wind the COG back a notch or two. Likewise you may be with a prospect that is advanced in their knowledge and application of your specialty product or service. In that case you can speed the COG up and move forward more quickly.

The COG also highlights the danger areas in the selling process. Those vital areas that, if you skip over, leave out or forget, then you are dead in the water.

Trust, belief, integrity, ethics and all other positive personal states are right in the hub of the COG. Without them, the COG shatters. The COG represents the sales side of the business machine. Be it large or small, it is the pulse of any company. It does not matter how big or small you consider sales to be unless you keep this COG well oiled and well maintained it will stop working for your bottom-line. Sales are the vital component to have running smoothly at all times. To look at it graphically, the diagram shows how the Professional Sales 'Champions Operational Guide' to selling stardom functions.

COG works brilliantly for any salesperson, from self-employed, to small and medium size companies, and for large multi-national companies, who want to reach Sales Stardom. The central hub of the COG represents trust, belief, integrity, ethics, and all the other intangible issues.

The arrows show the direction of the sales process.

COG Segments, as shown in diagram 'A':

1) Meeting and greeting, and building rapport.

2) The 'Discovery Schedule'.

3) Intensifying the need.

4) Tying down.

5) Preparing your tailor-made solution.

6) Giving your presentation, and dealing with your purpose written proposal.

7) Welcoming and Handling Objections.

8) Closing.

COG

Preface. **When Your Livelihood Depends on Making Sales**

Salespeople do not always close all of the prospects that they sit in front of. Nor do they always get in front of as many qualified prospects as they hope for or deserve. Worse, they do not close enough of the qualified leads supplied to them, or they burn the very costly leads from the lack of sales skills. This is not their fault, as many are unaware of the key elements that champion salespeople, having taken years to perfect, often jealously guard, and are reluctant to share.

For 17 of the more than 30 year's involvement in the sales industry I have had the good fortune to have been around some extraordinary top sales achievers. In that time I have had the privilege of promoting, learning from, travelling with, dining with, laughing with, sharing yarns, and socialising with some of the world's leading sales, management, and motivational authorities. Included in this list are such powerful speakers as Zig Ziglar, E. James Rohn, Dr Norman Vincent Peale, Roger Dawson, Dr Denis Waitley, Deepak Chopra, Wayne Dyer, and the fabulous Louise L. Hay.

Each has inspired me in different ways. The finer arts, special tips and techniques that I have gleaned from time spent with these champions have been incorporated into the system that I call 'The Sales Cog'. I have used 'The Sales Cog' system to help clients generate over $4.7billion dollars of business. I continue to use that system to this day in my day to day sales activities and have covered it extensively in this book. In that time, I have also taught sales techniques to many thousands of salespeople from individual personnel to smaller business right through to corporate multinationals.

Every time I observe someone in the sales field, or when I am on assignment in an advisory role, I pick up insightful nuggets that I also learn for myself. My sales qualifications and my own experience come from burning shoe leather out on the street, so the narrative reflects that background.

My three adult sons, now in their mid to late twenties, have sat around the dinner table or at the barbecue over the years hearing their father impart his sometimes unconventional wisdom, and relating stories of both my own and others successes and failures in selling. They have seen firsthand the highs and the lows that all those in the profession of selling experience over time. They are now, in their own way, involved in selling. I feel that the time is right to encapsulate my thoughts and experiences to share with them. This will ensure that my sons and other like-minded people gain every competitive advantage that I can offer them.

Each son is educated to a high level. The oldest son has a degree in International Business, along with numerous, maritime-specific, qualifications. The middle one has a Bachelor of Business Management, majoring in Real Estate and Development, and a Masters of International Finance and Economics. The youngest has completed a Bachelor of Arts degree to which he is now studying to add a degree in Law. Any edges that they can gain from my experience are not necessarily taught at university, but will help them in their own life plans that they are full steam ahead on already.

"The person who says it cannot be done should not interrupt the person who is doing it." – Chinese Proverb.

To get a job when I first entered the workforce the only criteria that needed to be satisfied was to be 15 years of age, so it was legal to leave school, plus a certificate to prove you had attended. National school examination certificate and a higher certificate for entrance to university helped a bit more. A university degree guaranteed a job. To buy a first home was around thirty thousand dollars. My first wage was nine dollars and seventy-five cents a week, and for an orphan boy that was mountains of money. Nowadays a degree is accepted as a starting point. Becoming employed is far more competitive. First homes are around three to four hundred thousand dollars, which makes it a lot tougher. Getting an edge is vital. Unless, of course, you have inherited a fortune like well respected business tycoon, the late Malcolm Forbes of Forbes Magazine fame did. In his biography Mr. Forbes was quoted as saying, "I made my money the old fashioned way. I was very nice to a wealthy relative right before he died." Don't you love that?

Selling is still a field of huge potential. So where do salespeople fit in the machine that is business in the twenty first century?

Segment One:
The Value of
Salespeople -
Street smarts or
formal
qualifications

Chapter 1. **The Business of Selling:** Until a sale is made - nothing happens!

Only by having everyone who communicates with the customer understand how the sales process works, exactly what each of their roles is, every step of the way, are you safeguarded against 'lost sale' disasters. The world's best accountants and administrative clerks can be in your business, but unless they have sales to count and process then they are not necessary. Cast your eyes around your place of work. Then, ask yourself the most basic of all questions in relation to business, "What do we need the most?" Please think again, if your answer is anything other than more profitable sales, because businesses are either expanding or going backwards. Business growth and prosperity is the pulse of the Nation.

Standing still is not an option. In the world of selling, no one gets a prize just for showing up. Either the sale is won, or the sale is lost. Winning, especially during a down economy; means only one thing, getting the sale.

> *"Running that first shop taught me business is not financial science; it's about trading: buying and selling." - Anita Roddick, founder of The Body Shop.*

It's time to recognise that the customers are the heroes of the business. The company will then become customer focused, and sales driven. Suitable administrators, and not the other way around, will then back up sales and marketing. To provide the best possible back up, anyone in administration should also have a working knowledge of 'COG'. The customer-focused salesperson then becomes the key person. And sales teams, with great back-up, then start to thrive. Sales teams are only ever as good as those backing them allow them to be. Now, before jumping down my throat, I am not for one moment trying to suggest that any role is less important, and I'm certainly not saying that we salespeople make great administrators, we often do not.

What I am simply saying is that making profitable sales underpins the whole business. The sales cog is a vital component, within the business machine, that needs constant love and care to keep the big wheel turning. Do whatever it takes to give the salespeople that special element known as the X-factor!

Here is how I see it. Just like there are, recipes for cooking there are formulas for selling. Attempting to cook Granny's favourite fruitcake without some of the key ingredients would be plain silly, the same applies in selling. If the key elements are left out of the recipe, often disappointment occurs. Getting these solid formulas and processes right should be given a great deal of importance. Then continual refinement and fine-tuning is made. Sadly, that isn't always the case.

All marketing dollars and all advertising and merchandising efforts are up in smoke, if the person who is selling face to face (whether this be physically or electronically) to the prospective client fails to close and secure the deal. Everyone has the capacity to be a salesperson; the problem is that selling is not a favourite task for most people. Many picture salespeople as greedy, unethical, unscrupulous individuals who go to any length to close a sale, and at any cost. The sales profession is an honourable profession, and everyone involved in a business must at least, learn the fundamentals.

Recently, a client of mine contacted her preferred freight company seeking a bulk rate for a large tonnage international shipment. A telephone representative from the freight company doggedly referred my client to their website for the rate. Later that day a senior representative from the freight company called to see whether they could proceed with a contract for that shipment. My client informed him that as their website bulk rate was completely inflexible, and the delivery was urgent, she had already booked the shipment elsewhere.

As a result of that freight company's failure to instil the core skill of selling into their telephone representative, it was an immediate loss of nearly $100,000. Including the incalculable loss of potential future business, that loss could be much greater. In only a matter of minutes, the telephone representative could easily have established the size of the order, the importance, and urgency, and asked for permission for one of their specialists to come back in five minutes with an urgent rate. Wasn't that an expensive few minutes? Imagine their total, hourly, or annual loss for the same problem reoccurring.

Salespeople, like customers, have indispensable value to the organisation and their input should be sought at all levels. Consider the structure of corporate business. It is now considered imperative for companies to have accountants, lawyers and a diverse variety of both men and women on the board. It should also be important that sales talent have a seat on the board as well. After all, non-executive board members can never be as well informed as they might hope to be on customer matters as the salespeople who are interacting with them on a daily basis.

The salespeople not only know the customer's needs intimately, but also know how those needs will affect the sales outcomes, which are so critical to company profitability. They are the ones who are out front doing the hard yards and often taking the flack for any problems because they are not always there to defend themselves.

> *"There are two kinds of people, those who do the work, and those who take the credit. Try to be in the first group; there is less competition there". Indira Gandhi.*

The traditional pyramid system of hierarchy and top down chain of command is dead in the water. That system has the CEO at the peak of the pyramid, then directly under that is administration. Then distribution sits under admin, with sales and marketing under that. The customer sits at the bottom of the pyramid. I firmly believe that it is well past time to up-end the pyramid 180 degrees, thus forming a funnel not a pyramid.

Great companies like Apple, Google, and Skype all know this. The result has the customer sitting at the top, with the chain of command flowing down; starting with the customer's needs and wants. Then sales and marketing sit directly under the customer, and then comes logistics and administration, and now the CEO sits at the bottom. Suddenly command and communication becomes a two-way street. That breakthrough achievement takes very little time, specialised profiling, or leadership expertise. Diagrams, 'B' and 'C' below give an idea of that concept.

Diagram 'B'.   **Diagram 'C'.**

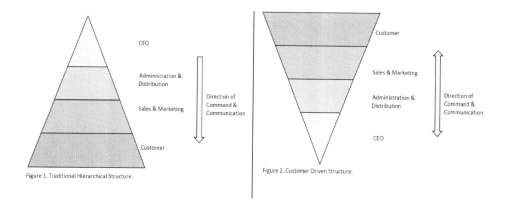

Figure 1. Traditional Hierarchical Structure.

Figure 2. Customer Driven Structure.

Chapter 2. **What's In a Title?** - Customer Optimisation Facilitator.

Heavy reliance on personal profiling has had a dramatic impact on the perceived value of a sales specialist. Emphasis has shifted; the trend now is to put a person, whose profile shows that they have the personality and skills to be in sales, into business development. It also highlights that they would be bored witless in a technical or administrative position. The position that they are then given is considered to be more important than a mere sales role. This is encompassed by the far broader description of business development. We now have business development assistants, business development associates, business development consultants, and business development managers. Relatively few seem to carry the title salesperson or sales executive. It's almost as though sales has now become the apprenticeship for Business Development, which includes a sales role, but demands a much wider range of expertise and tertiary qualifications. The Business Developer is also expected to be strong in other skills such as marketing, advertising, public relations customer relations, and product development.

The title of 'sales' no longer appeals to career seekers or the public. Or does it? Selling, on its own, can only offer a narrow career scope that perhaps fewer want to participate in. Maybe, they have the belief that people don't like being sold to. Nothing could be further from the truth. Perhaps this is a reflection of the old bygone days, when we were exposed to the antics of those social hand grenades the gold-chain wearing used car salesman and the guys selling the gold who wore white suits. I have friends in the car industry and they have solved that image now. I wonder if 'Customer Optimisation Facilitator' will be the next trendy title. Ultimately whatever the choice of title, the ability to sell and close a deal is the prelude to successful business activity.

The skill of selling must be a core competency and its one not learned in university. Like golf, a golf swing can be taught. However, to

15

perfect that swing and create a champion there is no substitute for going out, and hitting the ball thousands of times to develop successful memory patterns. Similarly, in sales, to perfect these techniques they have to be taken out into the field and used many times over.

Because of their size, small businesses have to take the same approach as bigger business does. There might only be one or two staff, but each has to succeed at selling. Make the solution to the client's needs their number one priority. Fetch the mail, empty the rubbish, purchase the stationery, and clean the work and rest areas, outside of selling hours. Improving selling skills will result in less work time; create freedom for more valuable family, recreational and relaxation time, as well as giving you more money and control. There is no luggage rack on a hearse, so you can't take it with you therefore enjoy what you've got while you've got it.

Having been involved in selling for more than 30 years, I thought by now that the art of selling to a systemised method and winning sales processes would be ingrained in every person involved in the selling of any company's products or services. With the masses of relatively inexpensive sales books, CD's, and the sales management material that are readily available today, no one should be allowed to start talking about, or representing, a company's products and services. Have them fully familiar with, and fully understanding the fundamentals of selling. Selling is a specialised arena, and because of the low cost of entry requirements, it is still relatively easy to enter.

All that is needed for personal appearance is; professionally-styled hair, businesslike but not necessarily expensive clothes, a few dabs of perfume or aftershave, some underarm charm, a good pair of clean, shiny shoes, a smart tote and pen and paper. Add to that, sufficient lunch money, a smile, and a reliable owned, leased or borrowed car. A fee paid open-book qualification or compliance certificate is sometimes required too, along with a standard police check. So the initial start up costs in the sales industry can be as little as $5,000.

Incomes of $150-$250,000 are not uncommon for better than average salespeople and up into the millions for the champions in the top echelon. When going into a business on your own, it would be difficult to find any business, for such a comparable start up cost, with such a high potential return. For such a low set up cost, it would have to be a very good business, even at 25% profit margin, that would give this kind of return on investment. Obviously, your first sale is selling yourself to the company you choose to sell for.

Speaking of first sales, it is often claimed that prostitution is the oldest profession in the world. Nevertheless, the 'Practical Physical Relations Demonstrator' first had to make a sale. Any negotiation teacher will tell you that she also had to negotiate the price for her services first and money change hands before the service was provided, because frequently the value of the service diminishes very rapidly after it has been carried out. Selling is the oldest profession.

Businesses have invested many thousands of dollars building up their own training programs and libraries, with the aim of creating excellent sales results. What has been effective and what is now happening? Recently I was invited to go out on a routine observation with a gung-ho, 30 year old salesperson from a highly respected financial advisory company. The company believed that all their salespeople were using their in-house set-script approach, in which they had invested heavily. I discovered that this was not the case; over time each had abbreviated or adjusted the rigid inflexible system to suit their personality, delivery style, mood, and time available. The effect was measurably detrimental to results.

Chapter 3. **<u>Setting the Scene:</u>** Experienced Observation Avoids Costly Flaws

To set the scene as accurately as I can recall, a salesperson, who I will refer to as 'Pat Black', arranged to pick me up in his car. We had agreed prior that I would be outside my office at 6 pm, ready for an estimated three quarters of an hour drive to the destination. At the appointed time, there was no sign of Pat.

Meanwhile, across the other side of town somewhere in a hotel bar there was probably another person on their own waiting to meet someone who had agreed to be there by 6 pm, as well. Had they been left waiting for more than say 20 minutes on their own at the bar they would, by now, have left. As it was 6:30 pm, I was thinking of doing exactly that myself. Just as I was starting to worry about how the pressure was now on for us to be there on time a car pulled over to the curb in the clearway.

It was a late model sports car. One of those sleek silver two-door models that salespeople for generations have loved to own, and one that screams "look at me don't I ooze success". The outside of the car was neither clean nor exceptionally dirty, but it looked uncared for. The rear boot lid flipped open, as the car screeched to a halt. The passenger-side window slid down.

The driver was a tall well built young man who appeared to be only a few years older than my eldest son; he was wearing a fine dark, sharp looking suit with colour-coded shirt and tie. It would be easy to identify a high performance salesperson if good looks and appearance were the only criteria. Sales managers would only have to seek out sharply dressed young men and women, and they would have a ready-made sales champion.

Pat immediately apologised for being late, stating the reason was that he had been held back in the office answering emails from other clients. Scattered on the floor were the remnants of several previous day's takeaway meal boxes and empty drink cans that were hastily pushed aside so that I could sit in the front passenger seat. I put my bag in the car boot when he had opened it for me. I complimented him on the amount of sporting equipment that he had in the boot and commented on how fit he looked. I was soon to learn what weight he can bench press, how many leg presses he does and how many kilometres he swims every weekday before work. He was also sporting a very trendy 5 day-old growth on his face.

In the car, I could very quickly see that he was right into technology. He had a satellite navigation system, on-board telephone, a laptop computer and all the technical wizardry you could possibly imagine. On the way, to the appointment we had ample time to chat. During the drive, he did not seem too interested in asking me any questions preferring mainly to just talk about himself.

Therefore, from the beginning, it was clear to me that I was in the company of a very confident salesperson. It was also apparent that in his own opinion, he was the best sales achiever in his particular state branch. His compendium featured a number of qualification certificates and awards that he carried around as proof. It was about then that wise old Benjamin Franklin jumped into my mind as I remembered his thoughtful line:

"He that falls in love with himself will have no rivals!" – Benjamin Franklin.

As we neared the prospective client's home, the car ran low on fuel. It was obvious that we were not going to make it there on time. Pat phoned their home from his car to apologise that he would be about 15 to 20 minutes late. This rang the first alarm bell with me. Punctuality is surely still one of the most basic elements of selling. He pulled into a gasoline station and filled the tank with $60 worth of fuel. Poor Pat, had to come back to the car and ask me to cover the cost, as his credit card had failed approval for that amount. He promised faithfully to reimburse me the next day. Off we went again at a great rate of knots.

We finally arrived and Pat parked the silver trophy right across the footpath. We were at the home of a 30-year-old woman that she shared with her mid 40's male partner. They had no children. We all shook hands, then Pat, without asking their permission took his laptop from its bag and set it out on their dinner table that they had seated us at. Glancing around the home it was easy to see what the couple's dreams and desires were. There were two large dogs roaming the yard where a fishing boat and smallish off-road type caravan were parked. There were two cats inside, that clearly had the run of the house, and they climbed all over us. The dogs were only locked outside for the duration of our visit.

Pat started the formal conversation, no doubt with the intention of building rapport, by telling this lovely couple that he had started out his career as a schoolteacher. As an observer sitting silently at the other end of the table, I saw the couple secretly roll their eyes at each other, silently saying, "Oh no here's a lecture coming up, how long is this going to take before we can make an excuse and get rid of them?" Pat had quite a sorry story as to why he gave up teaching. Meanwhile, I noted with interest that most of the time Pat kept his eyes fixed straight ahead, about half way up the wall glancing, only occasionally, in the prospects direction. He made no real effort to make eye contact with either individual at all. Once he felt that he'd established a bit of rapport, and without as much as drawing breath, he went straight in to his sales presentation. He told them what he does, what his company does, and how successful they were at doing it. He talked and talked. That great old-school salesman, Mr. Zig Ziglar, summed it up the best.

> *"Nobody cares how much you know until they know
> how much you care."*

Pat fumbled around for a few minutes, setting up his laptop on the table. He then opened a generic PowerPoint presentation that the company had prepared for all its sales team. From that point on, he easily slipped into his well-rehearsed sales mode and prepared sales dialogue.

The slides showed people just like this couple who had similar dreams and aspirations but not enough money to achieve them. Right there was a little built-in disturb which is good because you must have a disturb somewhere in your presentation. A disturb is a statement specifically designed to take people out of their comfort zone. My first boss used to say if you could ask a probing question that causes someone to lose sleep then you have disturbed him or her and gained that person's attention.

Neither, despite pausing at that point, did Pat attempt to intensify the prospects need. Nor did he endeavour to have the prospective customer put a dollar value on the financial problem demonstrated. He quickly reverted to the presentation.

The presentation slides were all in full colour and beautifully prepared. It was so commonplace and similar to what everyone else is doing, about the only thing missing was the old Simply Red song:

"Money's too tight To Mention."

How does it go again?

"So I went to the bank had,
To see what they could do,
They said son - looks like bad luck,
Got-a hold on you.

Money's too tight to mention,
I can't get an unemployment extension,
Money's too tight to mention.

I went to my brother,

To see what he could do -
He said brother like to help you,
But I'm unable to,
So I called on my father father,
Oh my father,
He said.

Money money money money,
We're talk-in' a-bout money money,
We're talk-in' a-bout money money,
We're talk-in' 'bout the dollar bill
Now what are we all to do."

The total presentation certainly covered a wide range of his company's products. Someone had obviously trained him to search for hot buttons, which means, something that the client opens up to and this was clearly the whole basis for his approach. Once he hit the hot button that described how much money they could save, he then reverted to type and very enthusiastically asked them to gather up all of their confidential paperwork.

Imagine for a minute that Pat was in your house with your spouse or partner having told you in about 20 minutes what he did and what his large, reputable company did. Now also imagine him asking you to give him all of your most confidential financial information and details such as your mortgage, your job, your budget, your age, your income, and other personal details. How would you react?

That is how they reacted too. It took Pat quite some time, and some convincing, using the company's reputation before he could even extract the most basic information. Then it took even more time before they could actually gather up the majority of the paperwork. In fact, they could not find everything. Choosing to end it there, Pat left them with a reasonably long checklist of paperwork that he required. He promised to pick that paperwork up as soon as they called him to say they had it all ready. He completely lost control of the situation right there.

Next thing, we said our farewell's and were both on our way back to his car. Tucked under the windscreen of the car was a somewhat unflattering scribbled message from the customers neighbour saying how difficult it was to get out of their own driveway with the way Pat had parked his car. As soon as we closed the doors of the car, you can guess what happened. Pat immediately started abusing his own company for the poor quality of the lead they had provided him. He erroneously felt that the client was so well catered for that they did not need anything he was offering, except for one product that may have saved them $1-$2,000 over the lifetime of their mortgage, or put another way about $3 or maybe $4 a week over the next 30 years. How valuable had Pat made himself in the eyes of those customers that night? The short answer - not very valuable, at all! Blaming others is always an easy option, isn't it?

Although I had sat there quietly observing, saying nothing much, other than hello and goodbye, I learnt something later from another member of the sales team. When Pat got back to work the next morning, he had actually attempted to put the blame on me for something he claimed that I had said to the prospect. Perhaps the customer who then hung a cloud of suspicion over him sensed this underhanded tendency. This in-home client meeting had been arranged by Pat's company. It had come via their comprehensive lead generating system. Therefore, the prospect would have had a number of phone calls from the company prior to our physical visit. There is no doubt in my mind, that the company would place a serious dollar value on the cost of establishing this appointment. In this particular instance, it was a visit to a private family, but the same sales rules apply to any sales visit be it business to business, direct selling door-to-door, in bound leads from advertising and marketing or to leads gathered by testimonial.

When Pat ever reads this book, he may conclude that I am just being a know-it-all, a smart Alec and being critical of him, because I was not initially overly impressed with him. I could see why his company wanted help for him. Pat certainly had a fine grasp of the main features of his product. He is paid on a retainer plus commission, so he has undoubtedly spent many hours in a training room being drilled on the features of his product and its benefits to the client. Ultimately, in reality converting the product presentation into a sale is the only point where money is generated, for the salesperson and the company.

I will be the first to acknowledge that it is always easy to observe someone else performing. I played my last game of rugby union many years ago but still enjoy watching a good game and from where I sit, in the grandstand or on a comfortable couch watching my television set, I have not missed a tackle, been offside, nor dropped the ball in the last 30 years. It is easy to observe and comment on others performance, but that is after all how we keep learning and keep up to speed.

Being observed allows for accurate feedback, which then leads to improved performance allowing salespeople to be the very best that they can. There is no point lying on your deathbed and wondering what might have been. Well-respected Australian Rugby League coach Mr. Wayne Bennett summed this up very successfully in the title of his book.

"Don't Die with the Music in You."

Mr. Bennett's book is a good, easy read full of anecdotes, inspiration, and homespun philosophies that he uses to build players into champions. The book also describes how he then keeps those champions winning games for him time after time. One key element that Bennett says he looks for is the size of the athlete's heart. The same applies in selling.

It takes real heart to be a champion because you can get plenty of knock backs whilst learning and perfecting the craft. Product knowledge is a vital part of the sales process, but in my mind attitude is equally as important. Whilst a good attitude should be completely entwined in the sales process, it is a different subject than just basic sales skills. An attitude problem is often harder and more expensive to fix than a basic sales skills problem.

From what I have seen, sales management often thinks that it is easier to change personnel than it is to change the person's attitude. They will go out and recruit a new person because changing attitude is a very complex and specialised thing to do. Often this 'attitude adjustment' is outside the scope of their skill set.

It is a critical art well beyond the old carrot and stick method of management to get a person to recognise that they have an attitudinal rather than a sales skills problem. It takes a good motivator to fix it in a short time frame. Lots of management take the short cut and fire the person with the bad attitude but often that just means someone else will fill the role with no guarantee of results. All it takes is effort and expertise.

Chapter 4. **<u>Different Sales Levels:</u>** Ensure your cream keeps rising to the top

Today, ample time, and resources, are misdirected, trying to develop poor performance up to at least a satisfactory standard. Analysis of sales shows that the Pareto principle, otherwise known as the 80/20 rule, still applies. Under that idea, 80% of your total sales are coming from 20% of your salespeople. Why then, is there commonly a substantial amount of time, energy, and resources focused on the poorer performers or the new recruits?

I recall, several years ago, a sales contest that a national sales director with a team of over 1720 salespeople endeavoured to apply, and perfect. The first year the manager gave a blanket attraction to anyone who hit the sales targets. They would get to go on a magnificent, exotic tropical island paradise vacation. On completion of this incentive, it was clear from inspection that the peak performers, who always see themselves at the top, won the trip.

The others did not because most of them did not see themselves as winners, and thus they mostly eliminated themselves from the contest before it even got off the ground. This section also got more and more depressed the closer they got to the deadline because they were getting further and further away from the target.

Management quickly discovered that they had taken their highest performers (who produced 80% of their total sales) away from the coalface, on a jaunt for two weeks. No sales had been crunched in that time. In spite of this, well-intentioned incentive program sales suffered dramatically. Those two weeks stretched into four weeks. People who go abroad on a two-week trip take a mental break the week before to prepare, and they take a mental break the week after they return. They spend that week getting over it and telling all their friends and colleagues about their various adventures and escapades. Those in the group who did not make the trip got even more upset upon hearing about all the fun they missed. The incentive backfired; the company had simply paid for an expensive celebration for its best sales producers.

Management then carefully analysed the pros and cons of that incentive. My team worked closely with them. From that analysis, in the second year, the sales teams were broken up into four different categories: Platinum, Gold, Silver, and Diamond teams. This allowed different salespeople to operate at different levels. The top performers, who were not necessarily all the same names as the previous year, still went off on the exotic trip.

However, this time there was less drinking and less golf. Instead, the company organised for an international motivational speaker to be present. This meant that by the time they returned home they were highly focused and invigorated. They got straight back into selling and sales boomed. The transition was incredible.

A target, that fractionally exceeded their personal past best performance, was set for each team. This way the incentive had achieved smaller incremental gains from each team member. By stretching them just that little bit out of their own comfort zone, the targets were achieved. That, after all, was the intention of the whole incentive setting exercise.

This proved to be far superior to lumping them all with one incentive as had been done the previous year. The ones that did not win the foreign trip still had prizes, commensurate with their level, to allow them to celebrate their successes. Some won prizes to wine and dine their partners; others received show tickets, movie vouchers and the like.

This was back in the mid 1980's when, as a relative youngster, I was first cutting my 'sales teeth', and I can rightly hear that favourite saying of the 'glass is half-empty brigade', 'but times have changed.' That exact same incentive program is still going gangbusters 25 years later. From what I see in the field of selling, the skills required have not changed that much.

A close friend of mine is currently the number one in a sizeable sales team. He has been all fired up over the past several months. His team management had put in place a contest where the premium is an exotic destination. Like most top performers, he does not like coming second and has put in a tremendous amount of extra effort to secure the award. Unfortunately, many of the others in the team have not been as excited. They all had input to select the prize and yet failed to reach their targets. It has been such a flop that the company has now cancelled the contest. Consequently, what they have now is an unhappy peak performer, with the balance of a team who has shown that they are not willing and able to stretch themselves for a challenge and win the prize. Vince Lombardi, the famous American coach and motivator of The Green Bay Packers said,

"The difference between a successful person and others is not a lack of strength, not a lack of knowledge, but rather a lack of will."

Incentives are a science, and for optimum outcomes are best implemented in line with a sensational motivator. Add to the motivator, a long-term planner of executive incentive packages, and 'bingo' you have a potent mix for longevity and on-going success.

There are different levels of sales. Therefore, different levels of sales skills are needed to match those levels. There is the salesperson whose company always has the lowest price. Then there are salespeople who only need to focus on the product such as a regular corner store. Then, there is the solution sale where the salesperson has to be able to provide a solution to the client's concerns. Being able to describe the features and benefits that the customer can expect is the first requirement. Lastly are the higher levels that require a lot longer to complete.

At this level, the sale is truly customer focused, and the sale becomes all about building long-term relationships. This level requires constant research, and even higher capacity, smarter salespersons are necessary. Then there is the level where the salesperson owns the solution with the client. This is the most productive and profitable level but also the most risky. In my case, I usually work with clients and share the risk on results with them. I have to make sure that it works for them; otherwise, we both take an unpopular bath. Obviously, experience and the field of endeavour have a lot to do with that. Someone who sells directly to households may experience difficulty adjusting to selling at board level, on a business-to-business basis.

The reason is that in an instant it is just too hard to adjust to the necessary wavelength to connect with the prospect sitting with that salesperson. The situation being presented in and the nature of the organisation also contribute. For example, someone who is a middle or line manager for a company during the day can be a decidedly different person at night in their own home sitting around the kitchen table. Especially when they are with their spouse discussing just how short of money they are from having sent the kids to private schools, and keeping up appearances in a neighbourhood that has always been somewhat out of their reach.

At night, in their own living room, that same line manager can be a decidedly different prospect to sell to than they would be during the day because of the environment and because of the possibility of changed status. Using the word 'decidedly' reminds me of Zig Ziglar when he brought his lovely wife Jean, (who he affectionately called 'The Redhead') to dinner at our place one evening.

He informed us that she was a 'decided redhead'; on further enquiry, he explained that one day she had suddenly decided to become a redhead. We all had a fond and memorable evening together. Selling at these levels is usually a matter of experience. It is exceedingly difficult to start a new salesperson at the top level. Let us now look at the key elements broken down into bite-sized segments.

Chapter 5. **Hit or Myth?** - Selling is a numbers game

Selling is no longer a numbers game it is now a matter of process. As a measurement of sales achievement, no one should care about percentages, as they can be seriously misleading. I could boast that this month I have had a 100% closing ratio. So what? In reality, I may have only seen one client, and closed them to make that 100% claim valid. Never be fooled by percentages. Like cricket or baseball, the only result that matters is the numbers of runs on the scoreboard. These numbers must be expressed in, either volume of sales or as dollar volume, preferably both.

Sales managers know that the top sales performers can often be the most difficult to manage. That is because we tend to be prima donnas. Get used to that. How do salespeople traditionally greet each other? "Hi. Nice to meet you, I'm better than you."

The extraordinary sales managers know that each person is truly unique and if treated all the same, peak performance is never reached. What you do is get to know them and realise how different each one is, then be grateful for these differences, celebrate them, and then capitalise on them! Just because, you light up in a certain way does not mean that your salespeople behave in the same ways that you do. Do not drive and motivate the way you do just because it has always been your own custom, think of other ways.

"You can't solve a problem with the same thinking
that created it." - Albert Einstein.

The same applies in any endeavour. The guys at the top tend to be the most demanding. In my experience, it is far easier to take a talented performer and turn them into a peak performer than it is to take a poor performer and even get them to achieve. Once we've instilled the consultative, professional sales process 'COG' in a company, in nearly

99.99% of cases the management will tell us that the only people who have had their noses put out of joint by our systematic sales strategy and methods, are the poor performers. We make no apology for that!

What habits must Pat improve, to go from mediocre to champion?

Pat had let me know remarkably early on that he felt he had all the sales training and skills that he needed. He claimed that he was already an 80% closer. When I asked him how often team leaders or sales management came out on calls with him, 'never' was the short answer. Management was always too busy either training new people or working on the database. Of course, that is a continual problem that sales managers have.

Because of time constraints, they cannot go out. The hardest sales manager to deal with is often the one who is leading the team but has never sold the company's products themselves. When out on observations with salespeople they can only give theory as feedback. They often overlook the little subtleties and nuances that can make a critical difference. In some instances, the sales manager has never been in a sales team either. Therefore, they certainly do not understand nor can they relate to the basic requirements of that salesperson's requirements. Pat should consider new ways to:

❖ Constantly review his skills.

❖ Ask for guidance from experienced heads.

❖ Challenge the client to bring the best out of him.

Segment Two:
Harvest Your Own Star Character Traits

Chapter 6. **Trust is the Key Element:** First, Last and Always

Trust is at the hub of all sales activity. Let's look at the absolute basics of building trust. It is a common mistake to believe that a prospect has to like you before they will buy off you. If that were that easy, then salespeople would just need to befriend a few people whenever they needed to make a sale. What is true is that people will buy from those they trust who have a solution to their problem. Put bluntly, you must be trustworthy. The job of the salesperson is to find out in a structured, polite, and methodical manner what these problems are, and how much they are affecting the prospect's future.

These vital, unseen, elements are the dominant intangibles of the sales process. They are the hidden factors that almost all salespeople from time to time forget. Nowadays it is essential to remember as these are the days of the Internet and of consumer scepticism. Everyone knows how to use Google search, and do. Either sell with integrity or find another career.

In my own consultative sales program, that I developed to train our own sales staff entitled 'COG', confidence, trust and belief is at the hub of the COG. Without them, the COG does not function. This COG is a tool that I have developed and keep perfecting year after year whilst being continually exposed to many selling situations.

The heart of it has been gleaned, honed and polished from sales techniques shown to me by real, true life masters of selling, being in the trenches using them and from books classic and otherwise. Possibly the book that has influenced me the most is entitled, 'No Bullshit Selling' by Hank Trisler. Another master sales trainer, who I have had the pleasure of meeting on several occasions, is Mr. Don Beveridge who gave me plenty to add to the program as well, and I acknowledge and thank him for that. The last time I saw Don, he introduced me to his son Dirk Beveridge and his married daughter Debbie Taylor. They are now both admirable trainers in their own right. Don taught me the art of writing proposals.

The rest of my sales skills were acquired the hard way over many years of selling, making mistakes, experiencing failure, going to seminars, having successes and watching other peak performers. Also, figuratively speaking, being slapped around, having the proverbial kicked out of me down in the trenches and on the coalface. I have no doubt that there is still plenty to learn. Working on yourself as though you are your own corporation is paramount.

What habits must Pat improve, to go from mediocre to champion?

Pat needs to recognise that the concept of trust is simply non-negotiable. You are either trustworthy or you are not. He struggles with it because he has gotten away with many minor lapses in trust over a longer period. Even the office staff accepts, and laughs off his tardiness. Now, those lapses have caught up on him and he needs to work hard to rebuild trust. You sell yourself to the prospect first, then your product or service. Pat should consider new ways to:

❖ Live up to his promises.

❖ Stop making promises that he thinks people want to hear.

❖ Start meaning what he promises, and can provide.

Chapter 7. **Sell Yourself First:** Feel good, look good, sell good

For male salespeople, facial hair should be out no matter how fashionable it may appear. There will be some exceptions; the fashion industry may be one. I cannot recall any top salespeople that I have worked with whose face had hair on, other than a neatly trimmed moustache. There are some notable exceptions to this observation, Richard Branson being one.

A University carried out some research on the subject of facial hair. The study detailed how they had compared defendants with facial hair to cleanly shaven ones. The defendants were observed whilst standing before a judge and jury. In almost every case, the jury had believed the clean-shaven person but had not believed the hairy person. Many sales orientated companies have adopted a corporate look with a dark suit, white shirt and tie for men and a similar colour scheme for women with a blouse.

That looks good, certainly a lot more appropriate than turning up somewhat untidy and poorly coordinated. The big watches and gold jewellery should be left at home for other occasions. Like tattoos, clothes and accessories are a personal preference. However, salespeople should look and dress to match their clients, that means the clients will remember what the salesperson has said and does and not just remember how they looked.

We once had a female sales manager who knew how to take advantage of her femininity and she consistently got tremendous results. At sales meetings, she usually wore only tight black dresses with fishnet stockings and high heels. For fun, she had a riding crop sitting on her desk. She threatened to use it with gusto on many an occasion on any salesperson not up to scratch. She would tap the sales scoreboard with it to very positive impact. The males in the group were either terrified or in awe of her, so very few came back without completed sales orders to the weekly sales meeting. That woman now successfully runs her own retreat for business people who are in need of a break.

Expensive looking cars can be a trap. Salespeople love driving them, as they are a well-known and recognised symbol of economic success. They are often the first thing that someone who has just made a big bonus immediately goes out and buys. However, if you are in that fortunate position congratulations, you lucky so and so, draw breathe and keep reading. About ten years ago, a mortgage broker acquaintance of mine, had such a good run of success in sales that he upgraded to the current model soft top Porsche. We met in a coffee shop that we both knew and he parked the beautiful beast right out in front to show all the other coffee drinkers.

It was white with a black soft top and looked impressive. He asked me why I didn't get one myself. Having a similar car once myself, my reaction surprised him. Affordability aside, I told him that I didn't drive a car like that anymore, because when I once had, at least one client said to me when he saw me driving in it, "I can see where our fees are going." After that, I went back to a more conventional car. Best to only roll the toys out in the weekend for driving and enjoyment.

Some 18 months later, I saw my Porsche driving mortgage broker mate pulling up across the road coming to the same coffee shop. I asked him where the flash car was, and he told me with a wry smile that these days it stays at home in the garage. He now drives a much more conservative modern four-door sedan for the very same reasons that I have just described. On the contrary, an old heap of a car will also be off putting because the client wants to deal with someone who looks more prosperous - unless of course, it happens to be a mint classic car, but the up keep can get expensive. Thank goodness for leased cars. Once you climb out of the car and arrive at their office or residence how do you greet people?

What habits must Pat improve, to go from mediocre to champion?

Pat should consider new ways to:

- ❖ Clean his vehicle regularly.

- ❖ Have a shave, as trendy can be scruffy in sales.

- ❖ Harden up and learn to take criticism as good feedback.

Chapter 8. **The Correct Approach:** Proper techniques for handshaking

A handshake is more than just a hello. It also conveys a message about your charisma and confidence level. Thus, a firm handshake is an invaluable tool to leave a good first impression. Handshaking goes way back to the sword fighting days when warriors wanted to show another soldier that they wanted to be friendly with them, and did not want to fight. They would stash their swords away and offer a sword-free hand instead.

Handshaking varies throughout the world, but the United States military rules seem to be the acknowledged universal standard for both men and women in a business situation. When facing the person you are about to shake hands with, they recommend that you have your feet slightly apart, and toes pointing out at 45 degrees. This should be from a distance that you can comfortably reach with your arm bent at the elbow, with your elbow still almost tucked into the side of your body.

Here, are the basic steps:

1) Introduce yourself prior to extending your hand. Make the movement of extending your hand at the same time as you are speaking.

2) Make the handshake and introduction brief and to the point. This should never be a lengthy engagement. Other people will start to feel uncomfortable if you hold onto their hand for more than two or three seconds.

3) You shake hands from your elbow. Shaking from the shoulder using your upper arm risks a particularly aggressive and jolting handshake. This action can appear overbearing whereas, from the elbow is gracious, and is simply a way of greeting and connecting with the person.

4) Never use a forceful grip. The handshake should be a pleasant, respectful gesture. It is not intended to show how strong you are. Use about the same level of grip in your handshake that you would use when you are opening a door.

5) Avoid the limp handshake. Nothing feels worse. When someone gives you a soft handshake, avoid the temptation of starting a power struggle by squeezing him or her back too hard.

6) Use your whole hand and be sure that you hold their entire hand, as well. Avoid gripping just their fingers.

7) Use only your right hand, provided you have one, especially when being introduced to someone you barely know. Have your hand extended so it is straight up and down, thumb up. Using two hands can send some strange messages perhaps too friendly or too overwhelming. Politicians often use this handshake, but it often appears artificially warm.

8) Make sure your hands are clean and dried beforehand. Do not wipe your hands off right in front of a person on your clothes or tissue. If they have, sweaty hands then discreetly dry your hands when they cannot see you doing it.

9) End the handshake after about three seconds or two or three pumps. Be careful to avoid an embarrassing, awkward moment in the handshake by ending it before your oral introduction ends. After all, it is a business meeting, not an intimate hand holding one.

10) If you feel as if you have made a mistake whilst shaking hands, don't worry. Cover it by making a quick compliment or ask the other person a question.

What habits must Pat improve, to go from mediocre to champion?

Pat has obviously never been trained to shake hands properly. He got through this opening gambit remarkably quickly. He missed a chance to make a positive first impression. He also introduced me but did not explain why I was there. Maybe he was too embarrassed to be truthful. In my experience if I go out on observation with a salesperson the prospect will think they have to support the salesperson, and it makes for outstanding results. Maintaining eye contact is essential to good communication. Pat should consider new ways to:

❖ Give people a compelling reason to want to listen to him.

❖ Understand that people love meeting others who can help them with their goals and ambitions.

❖ Clearly state what he will do during his visit and why.

Chapter 9. **Strong Eye Contact:** Engaging, unspoken connection

The art of looking people straight in the eye seems to be getting lost. In some cultures, a direct gaze is a sign of disrespect for authority and other reasons. However, in ours looking away from individuals can be a sign of insincerity and; therefore, not being respectful. The expression "he or she could not look me in the eye" may be familiar, and there are many songs and poems with that line. I feel confident, if someone you love was standing in front of you assuring you that you were the only one but not being able to look you straight in the eye while they were telling you these sweet words that you will agree with me on this.

"The face is the mirror of the mind, and the eyes
without speaking confess the secrets of the heart." -
Saint Jerome (374AD-419AD).

Next time you are in the queue for the bank teller, have some fun, and consider making eye contact with the cashier before it is your turn. Do not stand there waving your arms, do it subtly so as not to attract the attention of the security guard, local constabulary or a straight jacket. I'm not sure if they are trying to do it on purpose. They have certainly perfected the art of not gaining eye contact with anyone other than the customer right in front of them.

My two sisters and I used to play eye contact games when we were little kids. We would try to stare each other out. My younger sister Annette was by far the best at it and my eyes would always water trying to outlast her. It was a long time before I realised that she was not actually looking directly at my eyes. She was focusing on the end of my nose and, therefore, making it a lot easier for her to win the staring down battle. Try it. Chris Howard in his fine program based on Neurolinguistic programming goes a lot further into eye contact skills. I recommend his program called "Breakthrough to Success" to hone these skills. The recommendations I'm providing here are not affiliates of mine. I am just recommending their products and services because I think that they work best. When selling, it is not a matter of staring people down, but a matter of getting nice eye contact and that way you can at least get an indication of how it is other people are thinking.

As a salesperson, you do not want to be looking down on someone. Looking up to them is OK. You should try to keep your eyes at the same horizontal level as your prospects eyes. To achieve horizontal eye level contact, do whatever is practicable. If for example, you are tall and they are short then politely sit down.

Whenever we came back into the office from a sales appointment, a former boss of mine used to have a mantra for results. If the deal had been missed, he would say, "Did you shoot over the prospect's head or did you shoot at their feet?" However, if we had made the sale he would say, "So you got them right between the eyes."

Eye movement also helps to keep control of the sales process. When you want them to look at your presentation on the laptop screen, it is easy, just point to the screen and their eyes will follow your hand direction. When it comes time to complete the deal, you want them to look down at the contract you can simply use your pen tip to maintain control. Try it. Hold your pen down on the documents and their eyes will be on the paper. Slowly raise it up until it is in front of your own eyes, and their eyes will have followed the pen tip up off the paper and be now looking straight at yours. Do the opposite, by moving it down to take their eyes back down onto the paper again.

What habits must Pat improve, to go from mediocre to champion?

During our meeting, Pat should have looked the prospect in the eye more often. He stared about half way up the wall in front of him most of the time, only occasionally glancing in the direction of the prospects. He made no real effort to make eye contact with either individual at all. It was almost as though he was talking to the wall. He sells financial products, and it occurred to me at the time that this was an attempt to make an impression of authority. I don't think it worked, and rightly or wrongly, I actually felt slightly embarrassed for him. Be well mannered throughout. Pat should consider new ways to:

- ❖ Look people in the eye long enough to connect.

- ❖ Give everyone present equal attention.

- ❖ Nod when he gets agreement.

- ❖ Have a quiet air of confidence.

Chapter 10. **Mind Your Manners:** Mine your sales

Manners fit into this category; how to teach them tactfully to people in a training environment I am undecided. Parents or carers should have taught them when they were growing up. Good manners are another one of those intangibles that if ignored makes a tremendous difference to your ability to complete the sale, whether the clients visited are private individuals or businesses.

How rude mannered is it to fail to introduce yourself to the partner, receptionist or secretary? How dreadful mannered is it not to park in the appropriate car park? Throw personal hygiene into that mix. Be honest. What is your own reaction when someone else's breath reeks of garlic, their underarm has a strong body odour, their clothes smell of cigarettes or last night's hotel surroundings?

Take the time to check and ensure that you never have an unpleasant odour as a salesperson. Good manners should be a matter of commonsense. However, given the demands of political correctness they can be a bit confusing these days. We need to all be aware of political correctness these days and old-school manners are now considered by some people to be unacceptable, in certain circumstances.

Not long ago, when two women were getting into a lift with me, I stood aside to let them go in first and put my arm out to catch the elevator door open, so it wouldn't slam shut on them. As she went past into the lift, one woman huffed and gruffed at me mumbling that it was sexist to hold a door open. The other gave me a smile and a squeeze on my arm and thanked me for being so polite and considerate. As we were going up in the lift, the one who had thanked me spoke again to me. She told me that, in her mining company employee compliance manual, it is considered as sexual harassment if a male holds a door open for a woman. This applies, unless she has specifically requested this action from him. She also added that, at their mining site cafeteria, any male who offers to take the lid off a tight jar for a woman is classed as sexually harassing her unless she has specifically made that request for help.

Mobile phone technology has created a whole new, interesting collection of manners issues, as well. We have witnessed people using their iPods, iPads, or their mobile phones to Google what you're saying as you are saying it. Some salespeople might argue that you should ask them to stop using these devices when you are doing a sales presentation to them.

Personally, I understand this searching. After once or twice double-checking, and proving that what you are saying is true, they then tend to stop searching during your presentation. In my opinion if you had asked them to stop, they could become suspicious of your request of that and double check on search engines everything you have said as soon as you have gone. Poetic license is no longer an option.

What habits must Pat improve, to go from mediocre to champion?

How bad mannered was it, of Pat, to park across the driveway and partially block the neighbour? I thought it was an absolute no-no. In addition, how rude mannered of him was it to not ask if he could put his personal effects on the dinner table? Shouldn't you always ask permission before taking any liberties in someone else's space? Punctuality is a good sign of a well-mannered person who values others.

Pat should consider new ways to:

❖ Treat others with respect.

❖ Think ahead and keep the big picture in mind.

❖ Put others needs before his own.

Chapter 11. **<u>Be Punctual:</u>** The first tell-tale sign of how you value time

I just hate being late. It's a pride thing. When I say I will be there at 11.00 am, I like to be there at 10.50 am. Try to be early. Being 10 minutes early you can then relax, take a few minutes to tidy your hair, make sure your nails are clean, listen to your favourite cheer up music and start getting your head straight. The pressure is then on the prospective client to greet you on time. But on the other hand, when 10 minutes late, you have compromised yourself, you run the risk of looking stressed, flustered and so the pressure is then on you to start with an apology.

Either this also opens up the possibility that the prospect thinks you will rush, and maybe skip over something important just to finish on time, or you will rush yourself knowing you only have an allotted amount of time. Once you get into the habit of being on time, it takes away any need to rush during the presentation. A mad mate of mine has his watch set permanently quarter of an hour early to avoid being late. When people quiz him about it he replies that he is ahead of anyone else.

Client's sense when a salesperson is in a rush because it is difficult to disguise in your voice. Nothing is more off-putting to a client than a salesperson who gives the impression that they are in a rush to get out of there. For me, even if my car is over the metered time and getting towed away. Even, if I could be two hours late for the next appointment and potentially miss a sale. I will always give the impression that I have all day, that I am in no hurry and that I am there completely at the clients disposal and working to their timeframe looking for a solution to their problem. There is no sense in fragmenting or diluting your focus by looking past one potential client to another. Old wisdom correctly determines that you should deal with the one you are with and exhaust every possibility to conclude that opportunity first.

"A bird in the hand is worth two in the bush." -
Hand-book of Proverbs, (1670)

Plenty of salespeople mistake rushing around and high activity for results. Never mistake activity for accomplishment. I well remember a few years ago when every Friday afternoon we used to provide sales and motivational training for a major photocopier supply company where our role was to come in to their head office for an hour to rev up the sales team. To me, a Friday was not the best day to do this but their management felt that it was better on that afternoon than having them traditionally waste the afternoon over a long lunch somewhere.

The sales manager of that particular company was a stickler for everyone adhering to the company manual. Part of the manual spelt out that each sales representative should make at least 12 sales calls or visits a day. On this particular Friday, the top salesperson burst in late and apologised to us by saying "Sorry, I was on the 10th call and I would have got the 12th for the day but one of the bastards stopped me and asked me what I was selling."

The sales manager, who was present in the meeting, did not see the funny side of the statement at all. He took a very grim view of this reply whilst the rest of the room sniggered behind their hands and we all laughed heartily about it down at the corner pub later that evening. The quality of the sales call always beats the volume of sales calls. One great call a day can often produce more sales than you can handle.

When you are late for any sales appointment the person you are meeting is likely to think you do not value their time and thus they will be negatively predisposed to anything that you are going to say. Although your tardiness may have been no fault of your own, in your own mind the uncertainty about how the client is going to respond means, you are putting unnecessary pressure on yourself before you even start.

You may be thinking; that it is only a small matter of 10 or 15 minutes, so what? It is my strong belief that if you ever find yourself walking through an African jungle more often it's not the big Elephants that give you the most grief it's that little mosquito or that little spider that can kill you. The same applies in selling. Often the little things kill the deal. Failing to honour others confidentiality is one of those.

What habits must Pat improve, to go from mediocre to champion?

Pat and I eventually got there a little late but at least the phone call had given them advanced warning. Pat, when forced to make the phone call apologising for being late should have used that situation instead to soften the possible negative impression they would have had and turned that into an opportunity to build some rapport.

An apologetic call accentuates the problem and puts you on the back foot. For example, being careful not to sound glib, he should have sincerely said, "I am running 15 minutes behind schedule but can I stop and buy some milk for a cup of tea?" On the other hand, had the phone call been to a business client he might have asked if he could bring some coffee or a muffin. The objective being to take away any negative effects that his failure to be punctual made. His manager did point out to me later that Pat was habitually late. This is a habit he needs to correct and no one else can do that for him. Pat should consider new ways to:

❖ Be early for appointments.

❖ Schedule his workload more realistically.

❖ Make allowance for unexpected delays.

❖ Deal with one prospect at a time.

Chapter 12. **<u>Strictly Confidential:</u>** The evil of breaking their confidence

Once agreed as being "Strictly Confidential" and people are assured that no one will hear about your discussions without their permission, then that must be followed. Salespeople need to be wary of careless talk, often disguised as bravado. During World War II, they used the phrase, 'Loose lips sink ships'. Everybody understood it meant careless talk might provide valuable information to the enemy that may help them to beat us. The expression was a slogan during World War II as part of the US Office of War Information's attempt to limit the possibility of people accidentally giving useful information to enemy spies. There were several similar slogans all with the campaigns basic message - 'Careless Talk Costs Lives'. In sales terms, 'Careless talk costs sales and lost income!'

I had occasion to come across a family lawyer before he retired. We met socially through mutual friends. He was by all accounts a darned capable lawyer, but his greatest failure was alcohol. He used to take some unfortunate families' problems home in his head with him, and hit the bottle hard. However, I marvelled that even when he was so drunk he could hardly stand up, and despite people, trying to egg him on; he would never divulge any confidence. I commend this character trait tremendously.

Next time you are sitting in a cafe having a coffee just quietly listen to everyone around you talking. It will be surprising how many people are discussing sensitive matters rather loudly in a public place. The fact is, you never know who is overhearing what you say, and an excellent example of this was a salesperson not long ago boasting in the bar of a local hotel about a big client that he was about to close. As it happened I had spent the day training some people in the same industry, and a salesperson in the group I was with, picked up that valuable information used it to their advantage and eventually beat the talker to the punch and closed the deal themselves. The loud mouth at the bar is no doubt in another local somewhere boasting about another transaction that he is about to close.

Often when salespeople are gathered together in the sales office, they tend to like swapping yarns. This can be fun, but please make sure that it is not within earshot of a client that may be sitting in your reception. If they catch something they do not like, then you have lost both them and your sales commission.

Sitting in a sales office can be immensely tedious and can do a salespersons head in hearing some of the rubbish spoken among themselves by others. My preference is to stick around positive people whenever possible. I was at a sales place once and overheard two salespersons talking loudly about their previous night's conquests in considerable detail.

They went on, and on and I thought they must have been a couple of good-looking young bucks but when they emerged from the room, it turned out they were both well over 50 and well out of shape. I could only shake my head.

What habits must Pat improve, to go from mediocre to champion?

He badly needs to learn that merely saying that you will keep a confidence and then actually keeping one are two majorly different things. I later discovered that he had looped emails. His actions of looping the emails to others immediately broke that confidence. He should have assured the prospect that some others needed to be involved in the process and that the whole team would honour their confidence. Pat should consider new ways to:

- ❖ Think harder before opening his mouth.
- ❖ Realise the consequences of breaking trust.
- ❖ Make a commitment to be honourable.

Chapter 13. **People's Own Names:** Are music to their ears

Remember their names and profit. An American by the name of Billy Burden was one of the most impressive symposium speakers I had the pleasure of witnessing. His topic was "Building a Master Memory". When we first arrived at his seminar, in the morning, Billy was there greeting everyone personally as they walked in the door, he handed each person his business card as he listened to their names. Billy had only ever met a few of them in person before.

During the course of his presentation, Billy referred to every single person in the room by their first name, and he made only one error in a room of about two hundred and fifty people. This is probably the most impressive demonstration of a speaker "walking the walk" as well as "talking the talk" that I have ever seen. He deservedly received a standing ovation. Sadly, Billy has now passed away, but his stuff is still in production. Anyone can Google his material and it is very helpful to get hold of if you can. It is absolutely gripping information that you don't need to be an intellectual to use. I thoroughly recommend the techniques that you will learn.

Billy told us what happens to most people, when they are first introduced to another person. Most are so keen to get their own name and story out that they fail to listen to the name of the person they are meeting. I have tried to emulate the great Billy Burden and his master memory on several occasions using his memory system. The highest number I've ever reached is nearly eighty names. To master the techniques took serious effort, and they are lost when practice stops. It is a good way to make a favourable first impression on people. Even if, you scribble their names down on your hand to help you remember them, just do it. On one occasion, a sales manager from a big corporate called me and asked to bring his entire team around. His name was Ray Bell.

Ray arrived the next day with about a dozen of his associates. As he introduced me to the group, I applied Billy Burden's techniques then during the course of our meeting I remembered and properly used all of their names. Ray told me later over a few beers that he had won the bet at work having told people about my memory for names. He had a bet with them that I could remember them all and won it. That contact led to plenty of future work from the organisation that Ray represented. Ray also introduced me by referral to quite a number of other clients. I still think he is one of the best blokes I have ever met.

Memory for names all starts with your self-talk, which means the way you talk to yourself in your inner dialogue. So in this instance, for building a better memory, start by telling yourself that you have a remarkable memory for names. Say things to yourself like "People's names are important to me", "I remember names" and "I've got a great memory for people's names". Naturally, your inner dialogue is said in silence, or people around you will think you are a little bit odd. Once the recall of people's names improves then a far greater emotional connection with people in the first few seconds will result.

Now that you have remembered their name, you should also have a strategy that says something genuine and meaningful and shows that you truly care and want to learn more about them. Sincere compliments can get you off to a very good start. Perhaps there has been a positive newspaper article about them that you've read, or the business has a product that you love and so on. Just so long as you're talking about them and not about yourself. Use the word "you" as often as you can and keep the word "I" to a minimum and your sales results will increase even if you do nothing else. To go along with these good memory habits commit your presentation to memory by rehearsing and practising repetitively.

What habits must Pat improve, to go from mediocre to champion?

He badly needs to listen when others are introduced to him. How does he feel when others forget his name? Pat should consider new ways to:

- ❖ Understand the importance of people's names.

- ❖ Double-check that he has the pronunciation and spelling of their name correct.

- ❖ Hold his own story back until he has heard the prospects story.

Chapter 14. **<u>Enthusiasm Is Contagious:</u>** Ensure they catch yours.

"For every sale, you miss because you're too
enthusiastic, you will miss a hundred because you're
not enthusiastic enough." - Zig Ziglar.

Provided that it is not overdone, I think enthusiasm is absolutely contagious in the selling environment. How many times have you been in to buy something at a shop, met with an enthusiastic shop assistant, and then left with far more than you ever intended to get? Enthusiasm shows in your voice, on your face and in your actions. Seldom does anyone make a purchase of some value from a salesperson that is apathetic. Look in the mirror or have a look around the group and see how enthusiastic everybody is. One problem with enthusiasm in selling is that there is a very fine line between being enthusiastic and talking too much. The talkers always mistake telling for selling.

When meeting with clients, enthusiastic salespeople like a more informal style, the same approach used when having a chat with a good friend. For salespeople, this is the most effective way. The style allows the salesperson's personality to lead the conversation along by asking the right questions and, therefore, keeping control. Often you will sit in silence, while they give you an in-depth answer to your question. Never let enthusiasm revoke your ability to listen, know when to bottle it.

We have two ears and one mouth so using them in that proportion will enhance your sales potential. Try to practice your ability to simply pause and wait for them to answer the question because this process draws the best out of people. We often find that enthusiasm disappears in tough times and if left that way it can be the end of a salesperson.

My team had reason to be invited to talk to a corporate radio station owner, and after quite a lengthy discussion and analysis of their needs, we all concluded that, his team urgently needed a burst of enthusiasm. That might surprise you from an industry that outwardly seems to be pretty pumped up. We took the problem back to our team and then put a proposal forward with a solution to boost enthusiasm. They are a vibrant, fun, full on business so we included a few off the wall ideas to emulate that brand and business model.

We wanted them to all realise whilst things seemed down that we would soon rectify the situation and help them back, to number one. So the theme of our proposal was the sales team has a bad temporary case of the 'sales flu' and they needed a few days of 'sales and enthusiasm hospital' to restore them to full health. The radio station owner agreed to donate to the local ambulance service, and he bartered some time with a limousine company.

The look on their faces when the entire sales team was collected on the Monday morning in ambulances, and after a couple of days away at a nice, secluded conference retreat about an hour out of the city in beautiful tranquil, bush land was priceless. We had them taken home in private limousines, and they were all feeling well recuperated and inspired like multi-millionaires. That had been the focus for the weekend - The Extra $1 million Sales Campaign.

They achieved that goal easily over the next ratings period and had fun doing it. The limousine drivers picked up some well positioned clients work from the bartered, radio time and the ambulance people were very pleased with their generous contribution, so that was a win-win-win all around. You win, and I win is a great doctrine that champion salespeople and champion sales teams enjoy.

What habits must Pat improve, to go from mediocre to champion?

This sales call was, in fact, no exception to a typical case that many salespeople carry out every single day. Pat showed no genuine interest whatsoever. Please send me an enthusiastic salesperson any time as they can make a whole room light up with their presence, which is far better than the whole room lighting up with the lacklustre salespersons leaving. As soon as Pat had identified himself as a former schoolteacher, they were expecting a lecture and they got one. In addition, he quit too soon. He should have delved a lot deeper and seen how he could have further helped them. Pat should consider new ways to:

- ❖ Switch from believing that the world owes him a living, into thinking how he can contribute to other people's lives and businesses to make them more profitable.

- ❖ Consider the consequences of people missing out on the benefits of his solution and challenge his prospects to agree.

- ❖ Enthusiastically and sincerely, convey his message.

Chapter 15. **Space Invaders:** Be aware of personal space intrusion

By virtue of my profession, I have become somewhat of a professional student of people watching. Something that fascinates me is an invisible zone around everyone that we call 'personal space' and how people react within their personal space. The invaluable information that I've gained helps me whenever I'm making a sale or consulting to other sales and management teams.

Perhaps I will eventually become like the famous Australian horse trainer Bart Cummings who, over a lifetime, has developed an uncanny practiced judgment to evaluate, select, and train winners at the horse auctions and on the racetrack. Except that, I will be picking the human salespersons equivalent.

Personal space is the area surrounding a person, which they regard as psychologically belonging to them. Have you ever found yourself feeling like saying something to someone who is standing too close to you, "Hey you. Back off, you are in my personal space?"

More specifically, personal space refers to an area with invisible boundaries surrounding a person's body into which any intrusion may make them feel uncomfortable. Wikipedia has a very apt description of personal space that is worth taking the time to read to give you a better understanding of this. Edward T. Hall, who created the concept of personal space, introduced the notion of proxemics, (the study of the cultural, behavioural, and sociological aspects of spatial distances between individuals).

In his book, The Hidden Dimension (1966), he describes the individual dimensions that surround each person and the actual distances they try to keep from other people, according to subtle cultural rules. Different cultures maintain different standards of personal space. The amount of personal space one needs varies depending on who we are talking to and the environment. Hall has divided the distances of individual territory into 4 areas:

1) 0 m - 0.5 m: Intimate distance. Has this ever happened at work?

2) 0.5 m - 1.2 m: Personal range for interactions among friends or family.

3) 1.2 m - 3.6 m: Social space for interactions among acquaintances.

4) 3.6 m - 8.0 m plus: Public space used for public speaking.

That was done back in 1966. I would include at least one more that has occurred since then. That is "ATM range" (Automated Teller Machine), which is at least, 1.0 metre. Any closer than that makes me feel distinctly uncomfortable. They should close ATMs after 2.00am because nothing respectable happens at that time of the morning.

People tend to have an unusually strong, often negative, reaction to anyone they think is invading their personal space. The reverse applies if it is someone they love. Comfortable, physical distances also depend on the social situation, gender, and personal preference. The permutations and combinations of situations are almost limitless. In certain social circumstances, you get no choice as to what bumps against you. A packed public bus or commuter train at peak hour, for example. The importance of personal space in sales is significant and something that remarkably few focus on.

One occasion that immediately springs to mind, was when I was invited to do some work with an experienced Relationship Manager of a company in the wealth creation business. He was experiencing an uncharacteristic sales slump. The morning I first observed him was with pre-qualified prospective clients who the company had flown in from another state to spend the day with him. The husband was a tall solidly-built miner, and his wife was a petite primary school teacher. I was waiting in the reception area with them. When the Relationship Manager came out of his office and into reception the couple both stood up, the woman stayed slightly behind her husband.

The Relationship Manager, after shaking the partner's hand enthusiastically extended his arm forward, shook the wife's hand, then proceeded to pull her towards him, and gave her a hug. Frankly, the man obviously didn't like this behaviour. I was surprised, firstly because it was only their first meeting, also that the husband did not react more sternly with him for being so forward in invading his wife's personal space.

In my presence, the Relationship Manager then settled into his normal daily routine and presentation with the couple and finally completed and signed the contractual paperwork. The Relationship Manager then offered me a drink to celebrate. When someone does that I generally accept because it's a sign that they are satisfied with me and hey it's free. The following day, under a statutory cooling off period, the couple phoned in to cancel.

In an attempt, to preserve the contract and while they remained as guests at the hotel I went around to the hotel and met them in the foyer. They would not change their minds, and over coffee told me that there was something about the Relationship Manager they just did not like and it made them too frightened to continue.

When pressed for more information, I uncovered that the greeting was the biggest issue and it only spanned a minute or two of a whole day. There were other explainable issues, but that deal was unrecoverable. That cast doubt over the company's entire team. Right there was an overall loss to the company of some $35,000 over time. Make that same mistake 5 times and that quickly becomes a $175,000 loss, along with the multiplying effect of negative word of mouth.

Salespeople need to learn more about the importance of personal space and then follow the rules carefully because just breaching one element can make or break a sale. By way of light-hearted proof that may help you further understand, let's analyse a real life everyday situation. High-rise building elevators (in Australia we call them "Lifts") provide a demonstration and a fantastic opportunity to see firsthand people's reaction to their personal space in a public arena.

Many of us spend too much time each day going up and down buildings in lifts. So, next time you are in a lift, have some silent, personal entertainment passing the otherwise wasted time inoffensively observing how people do their best to keep their personal space even in confined areas like a lift.

Over the past 10 years, it has been my observation that lift behaviour has followed society and gradually become more rapid, less tolerant, and less respectful. It should be noted here that levels of dissatisfaction with elevator users tends to be in direct proportion to the height of the building, the number of smokers forced to smoke outside on the footpaths and the number and speed of the lifts. When the doors first open those waiting to get in used to stand back and wait for those inside to get out. This no longer seems to apply, and you almost need to fight to get around those racing to get inside the lift.

Picture this happening in your mind; you are waiting to get in to a lift, the lift arrives, and the doors open, the lift is not empty as there is already someone in there. Where is that person standing? Usually they will have their backs to the wall in the back left hand corner as you face them from the door. The doors close behind you and you are now both alone in the lift! Where do you go once you have pressed the correct floor button? You will probably position yourself to be standing with your back to the wall in the back right hand corner, and both of you will be looking at the lift floor indicator. The lift stops again, and another passenger enters. Where do they go once they have pressed their desired floor button? They go to the front left and then the next in moves right. On it goes, until the lift is full or you get out.

Now go back in your mind to where there was only the one person in the lift. How do you alter that seemingly unconscious socially acceptable order without doing anything, without touching them, or saying anything upsetting to the fellow elevator passenger? This is purely for the fun of course. To move anyone without physically touching or otherwise interacting with them is a skill that salespeople need.

In a lift, it is surprisingly easy to do, and a lot simpler than you may think. This time, you enter the lift, instead of going to your typical corner, try going directly to the back wall, and standing right beside that person. You can bet your house that they will move forward almost immediately. Expect a sideways glance when you do it. One person, when I experimented with that, once said to me, "what's wrong with you?" as they were stepping forward.

Alternatively, instead of moving to the back, stay at the front with your back to the door facing directly at them, don't give them eye contact or you may not survive to tell the tale. Do not smile or say anything. They will move almost immediately to the back right hand corner. Most of us know this personal space protocol but it is amazingly predictable, fun, and free to view. The point here is that social norms have a vast influence over our behaviour. All advertising agencies recognise that and they focus on matching product to social norms.

As salespeople, it is essential, when interacting with prospects and clients to be mindful of their personal space. To know that you can keep control of the situation and have people move in the direction that you want them to without necessarily having to say anything is an art worth developing. Remember these words to a song by Stings magnificent band "The Police" — "Don't stand, don't stand so, don't stand so close to me!"

What habits must Pat improve, to go from mediocre to champion?

In the dining room, the dining room table is decidedly much a part of people's personal space, and Pat invaded that when he placed his laptop on it without permission. The table is also a place that is supremely comfortable for the owner and they will be in the habit of sitting in the same place almost every time they sit there. If he was going to make an impact, he had to take them out of their comfort zone. As I detail further in chapter 35 titled "Study Seating", in order to get the best out of the presentation he should have seated himself between the two of them. There was sufficient room to do that. He felt they were a poor quality lead and that it had been a waste of his time visiting them. Pat should consider new ways to:

- ❖ Study human behaviour more carefully.

- ❖ Be consultative in his approach.

- ❖ Learn to stretch prospects beyond their accepted patterns.

Segment Three:
Prospecting -
There's gold in
them thar' bills

Chapter 16. **Qualify The Prospect:** Spend your time wisely

Up to 40% of the total cost of the sale goes into generating the lead and you, or your company, have already paid the bill upfront. This percentage, expressed as dollars gives an instant idea of why the focus must be on prospecting at least 40% of the time. This time spent on generating a qualified lead is essential. Unfortunately, you must put the work in first. Especially if you are a commission earning salesperson that does not necessarily, work for a week and then get paid for that week, then work for the next week then get paid for a week and so on.

With Commission sales earners, this work may take several weeks and sometimes months, before we get paid. Sometimes even up to six to eight months from the time when we made the initial contact and carried out much of the sale's work. Time spent prospecting, although it takes time to pay off, is well worth it. Cold calling sucks. I have never met a salesperson who genuinely loves it. To generate the appropriate lead takes various methods of prospecting and determined effort. Be prepared to think of innovative strategies that stand out from the rest of the pack.

These strategies need to be constantly reviewed and results compared against each other. You may never see the optimal strategy so doing anything is better than doing nothing at all. I have a friend who has done very well from prospecting at booths in shopping malls. He has specialist teams generating in-home appointments for household security devices. The best strategy is usually existing clients that will do repeat business with you. The next best, and least expensive are referral leads supplied to you from your satisfied customers.

Prospect and network, in a way that makes you become a valuable resource, as opposed to someone that is just continually badgering them for a sale. For example, I like to send the newspaper articles that I've read that may be of interest to them, or something relating to their favourite sport. That way, when I ask them if it's okay if I keep

83

communicating, the response is "Yes please." In my neighbourhood, every other day, at least one local realtor walks around stuffing flyers into everyone's letterboxes asking if they can sell the house or value it or tell you about a recent local sale.

A top realtor I learned about does quite the opposite. She asks people if they would like to subscribe to her free monthly newsletter. This newsletter details a number of basic things, in order to gain maximum dollars when they finally decide to sell, that homeowners should do around their home. Isn't that inspired thinking? With that one particular strategy, she has made herself a resource that people want.

To subscribe, they send her their name and details and ask her for advice, by default they become existing clients of hers. Guess which realtor they are more likely to choose when they finally come to sell their homes. On average, they probably do that once every 5 or 6 years.

Then there are those clients that you were not necessarily successful in closing the first time around. Maybe their circumstances weren't right or maybe they were not able to buy at the time for reasons they were unable to reveal to you, so it's always worth keeping in touch with them for a future time when they are willing to buy. Rather than bombard them with email and other things like most others do, please ask their permission to keep in touch and establish time frames that suit them. Otherwise, your communications start to become like spam that annoys the daylights out of people and then your information in a nanosecond goes into that whopping big Internet trash can in the cloud courtesy of the "delete button". Then you get blocked, and that prospect is gone forever.

When using technology such as emails, SMS and the like also use the social networks to attach that message to and then direct prospects to your business website. As previously stated, fingers hit the delete button very quickly with unsolicited email. People also say that they dislike having business promoted through their personal, social networks such as Facebook. It is best to have a business description as well.

The professional selling process 'COG' is all about building relationships, as opposed to making just the one single sales transaction.

Networking is another way of prospecting that needs to be in the salespersons arsenal. As a salesperson, network as often as possible. We used to gather at Commercial Travellers Clubs years ago and all stand around in groups drinking, and swapping leads.

Then after a couple of beers, the talk would turn to sales yarns and then girls and by that time networking was forgotten and camaraderie took over. Drink driving regulations have changed that, but there are now recognised networking opportunities in abundance where you can connect over breakfast and get a chance to show your product or service. Seminars and sporting events also provide excellent networking opportunities.

I shared the stage with a Mr. Joe Girard. Joe was in the Guinness book records as the 'Greatest salesman'. He sold Chevrolets. At sporting matches whenever the crowd stood up for a Mexican wave or to cheer, Joe would throw a bunch of his business cards high in the air. Many simply landed on the ground but with his record to prove it many obviously landed in the hands of potential customers.

I remember him saying that, at one dealership, he worked for early in his career, after only a short while he was so strong that other salespeople started complaining that he was getting almost every sale, they fired him. He was also always the last one in the dealership at night and first there in the morning. He came on stage singing Abba's "Money, money, money" and he sang it amazingly well. Training persistence like that into someone must start with the parents teaching it at a young age.

In some companies, leads are provided and in others, salespeople need to find their own leads. In real estate, small businesses, sole operators, often have to create their own leads. It is difficult and time consuming, so try to make prospecting as enjoyable as possible. Try new and innovative approaches and invest in a book on ideas for prospecting. Keep a record of what you have done and what has been successful.

Kick the daylights out of the successful approach whilst still experimenting with a few different ways for the days when and if that successful approach fades. Some methods last for years. The owner of a tremendously popular steak house down the street from our former office goes out religiously each morning after morning tea and puts his card including a 'special discount' offer under the wiper blades of every car park within a radius of about 500 metres of his restaurant.

He has done that for 20 years, and it never fails. You will notice that there is nothing high-tech, nothing expensive in that approach. He also keeps fit doing it, so that is a wise use of time and resources.

Mind you both food and the service there is tremendous, so his repeat business will be there, as well. Prospecting for referrals takes time. Work hard on ways to improve results. Focus your prospecting on a simple, concise message that encapsulates your product and service in one sentence known as an 'elevator' statement. This is an expression coined by North American sales trainers and simply means that if you met someone on an elevator you could tell them your statement in that brief time frame before they arrived at their floor.

They would know exactly what you do, how unique you were and how well you could help them if they were in the market for what you provide. The statement must be impactful and so filled with benefits that they would remember you and also refer you to others if they weren't. Be careful not to overstate the message when you happen upon people. I have heard people rattle them off at network meetings, and I think they often sound like contrived pre-recorded advertisements.

Meeting a prospective client within our lead description, somewhere unexpected such as in an elevator, I would rather greet them in the traditional manner, establish a more effective bond and ask them for an appointment outright. Use a hook to create interest. For me, it is an easy message to convey:

"We drastically improve sales results for you." When do you need more sales?"

Then hand them my business card with our concise message on the reverse side and state the same message verbally at our first meeting. To me prospecting is primarily about setting the appointment with a prospect, not trying to sell them anything, other than the idea of meeting with you. Save your elevator statement until your first meeting with them.

Stay positive and upbeat about prospecting no matter how tough times are for you. Arguably the greatest person I've ever had the privilege of sharing the stage with in 1986 in front of many thousands of people, was Dr Norman Vincent Peale the author of the book the "Power of Positive Thinking." He is still a legend in the professional speaking industry. He died at age 99, in New York, New York in December 1993, but he left behind a wonderful legacy of positive thinking.

During a break in the proceedings, I asked him about the most memorable positive action that he had ever taken. He replied that he'd been in a long queue in the great 1920's depression looking for work. He was, so far back in the queue that he felt he would never get the job so he wrote a note and tapped the guy in front of him on the shoulder and asked him if he'd mind handing the note up to the front.

Each person dutifully passed the note up to the front and when it got to the guy that was doing the employing he opened the note and asked to see the person who had written it and that of course was Norman Vincent Peale. When he got to the front, he got the job. On the note, he had written, "Don't hire anyone until you speak to me."

The best sales 'closers' in the world starve without a genuine well qualified lead. By my estimates, these leads take 30-40% of all effort and all budgets. We cover lead generating in our webinars and our intensive seminar and workshop models. Lead generating is the subject of my next book.

What habits must Pat improve, to go from mediocre to champion?

Any salesperson remunerated by way of a retainer plus bonus, and provided with pre-qualified leads should consider themselves lucky. Pat should consider new ways to:

- ❖ Treasure the leads more.

- ❖ Understand that the prospect wants to see his company's solution.

- ❖ Maximise the opportunity to help the prospect.

- ❖ Have his database working for him.

Chapter 17. **Help Your Marketing Effort:** Often 'No' is their only possibility

The biggest waste of time in selling is presenting to people who you then find not to be the decision-makers. Simply asking the person if they can make a decision is not sufficient. Very few people will tell you that they can't make a decision. They will usually tell you, 'yes,' but often 'no' is the only decision that they can make without the express authorization of someone above them, a spouse or a partner.

Should you still be getting long lists of unqualified leads, then, please support your marketing team (or whoever is passing you those leads) to better focus their lead generation success. Your goal in this step is to make the process more selective and automatic, so that you don't have to spend your own time eliminating unlikely prospects. Focusing too much effort on poor prospects can finally drive you crazy, so stop doing it. Just move on.

To borrow a sporting analogy, the salesperson is the finisher, the person who scores, the person who puts the runs on the board. In the case of a rugby team, the forwards have done all the work the back line has functioned like a dream doing everything perfectly to get the ball to the wing. At that point, everyone in the team is relying on the winger finishing. How often do we see a winger who can't finish instead drops the ball, and the team loses 50 or 60 metres down the park because of that lapse?

What habits must Pat improve, to go from mediocre to champion?

Not only does the quality of the lead make a tremendous difference in direct sales revenue but also in time management and eliminating frustration. In some cases, where the company is desperate for sales or maybe the market is dead they will lower the bar in the hope that they can create a few extra sales. This is the purpose of a database.

Pat blamed the company for the poor quality of the lead. He felt that he should never have been there and the company had wasted his time by putting him in front of that client. No doubt, the company had spent a fortune getting us in front of that lead. They had a complete telemarketing team and all costs related to that, television advertising, bulk printed material and lovely downtown offices, so the overheads must have been significant.

In addition, the cost to get the lead factored in would amount to hundreds if not thousands of dollars per lead. Therefore, it is certainly every salesperson's responsibility to give their real best efforts to try to close the business. Had the client not been qualified then Pat's grievance may have been a more authentic one. Pat should consider new ways to:

- ❖ Calculate the monetary value of each lead.

- ❖ Spend time with the marketers and lead generators to see firsthand how hard they have worked for the lead.

- ❖ Understand that the best closers starve without qualified leads.

Chapter 18. **Manage Your Sales:** Create a database that houses everything

Not all salespeople are renowned for being strong on record keeping. This is where a well-maintained semi- automated database, set to remind you to add certain predetermined criteria, is essential. It allows you to develop your own list for running your sales traffic, and it also allows you to create a sales pipe-line for periodic assessment and tracking of results. This means that you and your partner, manager or accountant can predict your sales results more accurately and with confidence.

Problems arise when salespeople offer optimistic estimates to their immediate supervisor, because that immediate manager will in turn pass those figures on to their superiors. The superiors will then have their behind-the-scenes administrators state that overly optimistic picture to those further up the line as imminent sales, with the knock on effect that everyone has unwittingly added to making the picture look promising. If, for whatever reason the salesperson cannot convert those sales estimates into actual closed sales everyone looks less than competent, as a result. Therefore, it is imperative that forecasting is reasonable and realistic.

Information to include in your customer database:

Please note that information is confidential and subject to privacy laws so check with your legal advisers about data storage before going ahead to ensure that you keep within the law. I have also found that it's a nifty idea to 'salt' your database, as well. This means that you save a few entries in there that only you know are friends or relatives with different surnames and some dummy details that can be clearly identified as coming from your database. This means that if anyone ever unscrupulously tries to steal your information source then you will soon know about this.

The prospect and customer database becomes arguably the most powerful tool to help increase your sales organization, so take your time and make sure you are capturing the right data. I suggest that you use a relational database, and contact management software, such as ACT, or ACT for web, to capture and record information. This way you can actually improve your ability to not only keep an up-to-date database, but also provide easy ways to access reports, lists and further streamline your ongoing marketing and research, and communications with your prospects and customers.

Here, are some suggestions for which information you should be gathering:

- **Key decision-makers names:** Include a key individual contact person's name. Also, watch for any key names or titles in the business and record them. This ensures that you have some points of contact of those in the decision-making process who could use your services. It also serves as a back up when your primary contact ever leaves the company.

- **Job title and job description:** Get the proper titles of any of your contacts; make doubly sure they are right. If possible, make notes regarding their job description and area's of responsibility. This information can be helpful to refer to later if you need to make contact with numerous people in the company.

- **Demographic and psychographic information:** Having a clear idea of the age, background, likes, and dislikes of your prospects or customers can be decisive in improving communication with them. As you have discussions with your contacts, if they express elements of their background, experience, or if you can calculate some information from this observation, make some notes in your database. Many times, especially with prospects, it's useful to have these notes on hand to refresh your memory of these details before making the next follow-up contact.

- **Company name:** Be sure to get the correct spelling and format of the company, so that it will appear right on all of your letters, faxes, email and other correspondence. Pay close attention to these details, as making a mistake can make for lousy presentations later in your communication to a prospect or client.

- **Addresses:** Get both the physical and the mailing address if they are different. Ask them and then make a note of which address they prefer you to send them anything.

- **Acceptable methods to contact them:** Include any alternative ways to contact the customer such as fixed phone numbers, mobile phones, email addresses, website address, fax numbers, and Facebook. As the relationship evolves with the prospect, or client, be sure to update the database when new ways to potentially contact them become apparent.

- **Purchasing history:** Keep notes of the date of the first purchase, subsequent services, amount of sale and any other information from those transactions.

- **Source of lead:** If the contact is a prospect, be sure to keep track of how the customer originally made contact with you. Which came from another client's referral? From a direct mailing, you did. Alternatively, did the lead come from a booth at a conference or trade show? Code this event into your database for later reference.

- **Source of sale:** When the prospect makes their first purchase, have the database remind you to record any source that they may have responded to. Did they respond to an email or follow-sales letter you sent? Or, did you make a phone call or personal visit? Tracking this information over time helps you to understand what methods of follow-up are the most effective in generating first-time revenue from a prospect.

- **Any specific client needs:** Capture and record any specific needs that the prospect or customer indicates to you as part of your ongoing dialogue with them. This is valuable information that can be used later to extend or revise your service offerings.

- **Client remarks:** Be sure to keep track of any comments from clients, whether they are complaints, testimonials, or unique requests. Make sure to record any pertinent details on their payment history.

- **Relationship building:** The database can also identify a raft of issues that you wouldn't otherwise think of, or retain such as; client birthdays, memberships of buying groups, industry category, and associations. These and other useful things are what help you build client profiling. This client profiling will help you to make an ongoing relationship that keeps client's buying from you in the future.

- **Other matters:** Your database can also be used to provide; Status reports, Variance reports, Key performance indicators, GANTT charts, Milestone charts, and cost control schedules.

Selling is a process, so the database should be set up to mimic this process and give you highly accurate feedback. Databases are not just about quantity. Forget the past theory that sales are all about numbers. Sales managers used to rabbit on about sales just being a numbers game. To me that is rubbish. If you see one person, even if they are highly qualified as a prospective client but you can't close them either you lack the facts about your product or you require selling skills. So unless, you are relying solely on luck, your results will be the same for 100 prospects if the same mistakes are still being made. You will still get zero sales.

> *"Rely on the rabbit's foot for luck if you like, but remember it didn't work for the rabbit." - Charlie 'Tremendous' Jones.*

To me, a sales process is a science and it is all about the elements, and steps that you take in defying them to say 'no,' and then getting them to 'yes.'

Segment your database: Your database will also allow you to balance your sales activities more accurately. Each element of the process is intrinsically linked, so it is necessary to split your database categories into segments that determine where your prospects are; and the possibility of getting them and the potential profit from each sale. You can also see where you need to become stronger. For example, if your prospecting segment is booming and they are highly qualified, but your sales are down then the database shows the problem area. Maybe it will show that you haven't done enough final presentations so then you can work harder on developing and perfecting that segment. Measure as many segments of the sales cog as you possibly can. You will then be able to see an instant picture of how you are tracking at any given time.

Use the database also to help establishing goals and benchmarks, so it acts as a measuring device that keeps you accountable to yourself and fired up to achieve your goals. Databases are remarkably labour intensive and time consuming to build. Maintaining them can also be expensive, as the business world tends to be fast flowing and key people move about. Monitoring them can be time consuming. Every company and every IT expert has their own opinion about which database is best. For some purposes - Microsoft Outlook and Excel suite are just fine. Our own IT engineers have set up a brilliant ACT-Sage in the cloud database to send us all calendars, and reminder SMS's to our mobile phones. The system will even ring an alarm to remind us of the appointment – all very standard stuff. They have also incorporated a template so that filling in the details is easy. The devil is in the detail.

In my experience, many companies protect their sales and marketing databases too much. Years ago we realised the extent of effort, time and investment needed to maintain an extensive database, eventually we hit on the idea of sharing our data and customer base with other companies that we trusted, obviously in different types of businesses than ours. We formed a marketing alliance so that we could bundle several offers into one and then all share our upgrades and changes. Yes, you do have to be fully within all privacy laws and carry out these transactions ethically.

Whilst doing all these management tool activities, remember to build in some family, relaxation, and recreational time for yourself. After all we are trying to enrich our lives. Take into account that you also have to allow for travelling time, waiting time at appointments, chasing up others, handling problems and doing your paperwork. All of these take time. Champions always look as though they have more time. That is because they are well organised and well disciplined.

What habits must Pat improve, to go from mediocre to champion?

Pat never took the time to ask for the accurate spelling of his prospects names. He did not note down the dogs and cats names. Remember they were without children. It is therefore, safe to assume that the animals were their family particularly, as they had the run of the house. Pat should consider new ways to:

- ❖ Be more observant, for clues that are everywhere.
- ❖ Be more thorough in his preparation.
- ❖ Dot the I's and cross the T's.

Segment Four:
Now You Are At the
Initial Appointment

Chapter 19. **It's All About Them:** Leave your baggage in the car.

When they were younger, our three boys loved having a Jeffrey Archer short story read to them. This is a wonderfully constructed human story entitled, 'The Grass is Always Greener', from his book 'To Cut A Long Story Short.' The story is all about people, their worries and the baggage that they are forced to carry from the context of their lives. It was based around a downtown building and had all the intrigue and problems known: embezzlement, adultery, sex, loneliness, rejection, greed, and fraud.

A typical example of work by Jeffery Archer, interesting, enthralling and entertaining. The story begins outside the building of a large institution, where a tramp lived and described his worries. It tells how, at first light, he has to be gone before the concierge arrives with all his worries.

After that as others arrive, we hear their problems and so on until finally at nine o'clock the CEO, whom you would think that life was peachy, turns out to have more problems than all the rest of them. The story had the reader re-examining their own circumstances and probably realising that there are enviable situations in your life.

Imagine if you were invited to a, 'swap all your problems with someone else' party where everyone would put their problems in the middle of the room and then you could take home any person's problems that you preferred. I feel sure that after only a few minutes of sitting around and hearing everybody else's problems you would gladly jump into the middle, get your own problems back, and get the heck out of there. It is also true for salespeople and clients alike. We all have problems. Some of us may have lost their parents at an early age, or never known them. Some may have been divorced. Some have little or no money. Others have children who won't talk to them, spouses who hate them. Others have superiors that they are continually at loggerheads with. These problems are intensely real, and can be heart wrenching.

To function at a peak performance level, get into the habit of leaving personal problems in the car before going to a sales appointment. Wrap them up in a small imaginary plastic bag and instruct them to wait there. Believe me, they will still be there to greet you when you return to the car. During the sales presentation, as a 'solution finder', the only problems to be focused on are those of the clients. The client does not want to hear about yours. Because our role is to find and offer solutions, we should treat those clients' problems with empathy and not sympathy

While with your prospect, do as the actor Michael Caine suggested: "Be like a duck. Calm on the surface, but always paddling like the dickens underneath." Generally, if you have had a successful sales call that has made you some money, then they will appear to be in a slightly smaller bag when you get back. To attempt to list down all the attitude and mental block type things that are discouraging us, and holding salespeople back could take forever. Here are a few I have heard of, that might be encountered.

Being in a cold personal relationship.

Being the parent of kids, who are giving you distress.

Having failed in a small business.

Being made redundant.

Had an illness or personal injury.

Being broke.

Lost your home through bank foreclosure.

Being negative.

Unable to relax.

Unable to sleep.

Overstressed and worried.

Feeling of hopelessness.

Midlife crisis.

Old-age catching up.

Family member, loved one, or friend dying.

Shattered dreams.

Having a boss who disagrees with you.

Lacking a clear focus.

Wishing you were someone else.

Being impatient.

Reading media on a daily basis about the bad economy.

Watching the news and hearing about the 1% who commits crimes.

Lack of confidence in yourself.

Lacking confidence in those around you.

Regretting past mistakes.

Holding on to lost love.

Hiding in your comfort zone.

Letting your personal agenda suffer such as health and fitness.

Fearing rejection.

Lack of assets and resources

Not having enough superannuation to retire.

Feeling that you lack the skills or the motivation to take on a new challenge.

Feeling lacklustre, or suicidal.

Dwelling on past failures.

Having unpaid bills and threatening creditors.

In need of automobile repairs.

Having to move houses.

Owing the tax department.

And so on. I am sure you get the picture. Try your own list, but be real selective about who you share it with so it does not become a whip for someone else to use across your own back.

What habits must Pat improve, to go from mediocre to champion?

Pat has to let go of his old school teaching days. His lengthy account of giving up school teaching added nothing to explain how he was going to be the client's problem solver. It takes real confidence, belief, faith, awareness, patience, and persistence to deal with these adverse matters and to overcome them. Once you have, do not become over confident. I have watched salespeople who are over-confident and seen how the prospect has considered them arrogant, aloof, and a bit insensitive to their needs. Being overconfident is a trap that you should avoid. Stop yourself from getting cocky, because if you don't the universe has an uncanny knack of balancing matters for you. Pat should consider new ways to:

❖ Know that people trust schoolteachers. Therefore, it is worth briefly mentioning.

❖ Keep his explanation brief.

❖ Focus on the prospect to give them reassurance that he really cares about them.

Chapter 20. **Establish A Connection:** Create a bond and confirm they qualify.

Many sales representatives that I have accompanied at their company's request as an observer look around the prospective client's home or office for a photograph. They then spend time enquiring about the subject of that photo. Often it is a family photograph. Personally, I believe this is risky because it is being too close too soon. Moreover, you run the risk of there being a family issue or worse yet a family tragedy and the picture is there as a keepsake.

With business-to-business sales, I try to avoid using the 'look in photos' way, or anything else. I know business people recognise this method as other salespeople use it every day. In someone's private residence, it is different and more necessary to build rapport before you try to connect. Walking into someone's office also gives you many clues as to the type of language that they primarily use to communicate.

Listen to, and note, the words they are using. They will fall into one of three types: seeing, hearing or feeling. 'Seeing' people will have piles of newspapers, magazines, and stuff like manila folders all around the office. Perhaps they will have a pegboard with sticky notes or pictures stuck to it. Those who are, 'feeling' will surround themselves with pictures of family and friends.

Maybe they will have drawings from their children or grandchildren. Look for keepsakes and trophies. Then, 'hearing' people generally have their office all neat and tidy. Once you pick their type, start matching their language, as quickly as you can. Speak at the same speed, in the same voice tone and volume.

Building rapport can be hazardous because most salespeople do it and therefore, it is easily recognised as a sales technique. Get this wrong, and you will not establish a trusting relationship with your prospect.

Instead, they will get the impression that you are just trying to control or manipulate them in an attempt to sell something to them.

Anyone who feels manipulated will be distrustful of your intentions and, no matter how sincere, they will never want to connect with you. When dealing with business prospects I want the client to know three things very early in the discussion. Firstly, that I appreciate them giving me their valuable time. Secondly, that I am there primarily to listen to them. Thirdly, I want them to know that best business practices will be followed at all times.

When I do think the situation needs some rapport building, I have found the thing people most like to talk about is themselves, and their sport or hobbies. Therefore, I prefer to do my homework, and research the prospect before I set out for the appointment. I do a Google search on the company and the person. In addition, if it is a business I may read the annual report or any related newspaper articles. I am not someone who is seeking to dig up anyone's past deep, dark, dirty secrets. They are of no interest to me.

What I am after is a clearer picture, or things that we may have in common, in an effort to choose the best ways to connect with them towards building a mutually beneficial relationship. On the first visit, I use my peripheral vision to look for any obvious signs of a sport or hobby and then if I think that I need to discuss those sports or hobbies, I will, at the appropriate time. Avoid scanning the room as it makes you seem nosey and is not a good look at the outset.

Very rarely does a prospect ever say to me, "Look I'm sorry I just do not have time to talk about my hobby or sport". Frequently they are impressed that I ask about them personally, without being invasive. There have been several occasions, where I have commented on the photos of their racehorse, boat, racing car, or golf tournament, and then subsequently been invited out to join them. When that sort of invitation is made you know you have built invaluable rapport and connected on a meaningful level with the prospect and it has only actually taken a few minutes. The sale will go in and out of rapport so keep rebuilding it all the way through.

Once a level of rapport has been established, then I begin at the start of the sales COG. Progressing to 'identifying the need' and following the COG right through progressively to the end. I know the steps well; they are a remarkably straightforward and easy to learn. A method that gives me a clear picture, in my head, as to exactly where I'm at in the sale. Many sales trainers suggest starting with a closing question and that you should 'always be closing' during your presentation.

The acronym for "always be closing" is the old 'ABC' of selling principle. My opinion is that unless you 'open the sales process' well then you cannot possibly close well. The reverse also applies. If, you close too soon and fail, you have not opened properly. 'ABC' to me means, 'Always Be Closing' your prospect on the idea of taking the next step in the sales COG.

As an example, of the old ABC method, one of my ex employers was the owner of a fair sized construction company. We became firm friends. His sales skills had been honed many years earlier in a hard, old-school environment called the 'University of Hard Knocks'. He had owned his own manufacturing company, but a bigger challenge appealed to him. He had decided to branch into property development and residential construction. He purchased a large block of land, under a 'put and call' option. The land was near the ocean on the east coast of Australia, in the days before the sea change mentality made them very expensive. During the weekends, he would take his very understanding wife in their luxury caravan and park it on the site. Out on the main highway, he would put out several large A-frame signs advertising, "Fresh crab sandwiches - absolutely FREE!"

His wife made the lovely, fresh crab sandwiches in the caravan while he sat under the awning at the front, waiting for prospective clients to drive up, having carefully followed the solid arrows on his signs to the site. Usually it was a young couple looking to build their first home. As they pulled up in front and the wife, or partner, climbed out, my boss would yell out to the driver, "Bring your cheque-book mate so while my wife makes your girl a free sandwich you can buy her a new home." That is a closing statement right from the first moment of contact. No rapport building, and at that point, he just got straight into their needs and wants!

Last time I encountered him, he had personalised number plates on a late model Rolls Royce, so the ABC techniques appeared to have worked well for him. He was a hard act to follow, though as he was in his early 50's he seemed to get away with a lot more than younger salespeople might. His adventures could fill another book. Sometimes, being direct and straight to the point can produce remarkable results.

One successful sales assignment where we shared ownership of the outcome with the client came from my habit of scanning through the newspapers, and the internet, to see who was advertising for salespeople, and what they required of them. The advertisement was of medium size with a solid border with the bold heading, "Closers Wanted!" The only other words were a name and number to call. It was concise, so I took the same approach. I called and when the person named in the advertisement picked up the phone I just said, "When do I start?" He responded with excitement in his voice saying "A closer. How soon can you come over? "

When I arrived in his office, he told me that he did not want me to close any sales for them. Instead, he preferred that I teach their entire sales team how to close like that. They had nearly one hundred sales representatives across the country. You can appreciate that we broke out the bubbly that night.

What habits must Pat improve, to go from mediocre to champion?

Pat also rushed past and missed this crucial stage of building rapport. He was far to keen to jump into his presentation speech. He never took time to connect with them by focusing on their needs, so he could help them get what they wanted. The deepest human motive is the desire to feel valued, appreciated, and important. The key to connecting and winning others over is, to make them feel significant. Pat should consider new ways to:

- ❖ Take time to get know people.

- ❖ Demonstrate that his solution is not simply a one size fits all, but is tailored to suit their unique requirements.

- ❖ Keep reminding himself that 'telling isn't selling'.

Chapter 21. **Be Direct:** Let them know exactly why you are there.

I think that the salesperson should inform the client why they are there. Be truthful. Say, "Ultimately I would like to have your business so what I'm here today for is to find out what I have to do to earn that business. Is that okay?" Thus, you have summarised why you are there, built some trust and trial closed all in one short sentence right at the outset.

By the time, this point is reached, 30% to 40% of the budget has been spent to put you in front of that prospect. Salespeople owe it to themselves, and everyone else to put on the best performance for that prospect that they possibly can. The prospect deserves to see you at your finest and you should make every effort possible not to disappoint them.

That is why it is necessary to continually hone and revise the presentation until it is perfect. Once you have perfected your presentation be reluctant to make any changes. Only make minor refinements. The basis for most salespeople changing their presentation is that they get bored with repetition.

Therefore, they change it. Imagine how dismayed you would be if you heard your favourite song of all time sung with the words having been changed. It just would not seem right would it? Remember, your prospect has never seen your presentation before, unless they are repeat business. For this, you pull out your 'repeat business' presentation. Ideally, you will have four or five specific presentations in your mind to remember and use in the appropriate situation.

Consider yourself to be just like an acclaimed stage performer who comes out night, after night, repeating exactly the same words every time. They use the same punch lines, the same timing, the same everything. During the day, whilst they are not with an audience they practise that script over, and over again. Repetition helps to make powerful presentations.

111

Think how long the leading shows run on Broadway and how long those perfect scripts continue to enthral the audiences. Each night they have a different audience, just as you a salesperson have a different audience most times you perform. Those who have gone back to experience the show again know that they are going to hear exactly the same words and yet they still love it.

All top salespeople use exactly the same techniques as those famous actors have rehearsed, tested, tried, perfected, and then repeated over and over again. Have several different "songs" for whenever the occasion requires because not every sale is the same. Once rehearsed every salesperson in the organisation is then singing off the same song sheet. Say one salesperson was to lose their voice halfway through a presentation then another should be able to step in and pick up without missing a beat.

The song that you sing and the stories you tell must relate to the customer. It must also connect with the solution to their needs and wants, using the vocabulary that they can easily understand. Selling is not an academic activity. Nor is it a theoretical examination, so you do not need to use fancy words. Use words that convey the impression that you have a firm grasp, and understanding of, language, with no personal bias. The customer subconsciously feels happy when you are both in harmony.

A sales representative from a reputable worldwide business supplier called on me once and told me that if I went ahead he would win a trip to Fiji, as he only needed one more sale. His presentation never connected with me, as I had no interest in him going on vacation at my expense. He left my office shortly after still needing that one more deal to be awarded the trip prize.

The skill is to change the prospect's opinion away from thinking of you as just another salesperson with a product or service that you are trying to flog, into believing that you are a remarkable person in their mind who has exactly what they need and who they would like to buy from right now. Unless you honestly and sincerely believe exactly that then find another product or company to represent that you do believe in, or get another occupation. Selling just isn't for you. This is a significant step so spend time perfecting it.

There is a problem with being perceived as there to 'sell'. Here is the problem. Just like some economists seem to hate using the 'R' (recession) word, it strikes me that these days salespeople and business leaders seem to find it extremely difficult to use the 'S' (sell) word preferring instead to tip-toe around the point with terms like increased growth, improved ROI and bottom line. What they actually mean in every day non-corporate speak is, "we need more sales at the right margin."

The basics we have covered so far classically fall into this category. If you are punctual, that helps build trust and belief. If you look and act professionally, that helps to build trust and belief. Then, if you state your reason for being there that helps build more trust and belief.

What habits must Pat improve, to go from mediocre to champion?

During the review session, the next morning Pat acknowledged that he probably had been told all the sales skills, by trainers within the organisation but did not use them enough. He could not explain why he had changed his approach, but clearly understood the need to improve urgently. His credit card had been rejected for $60 worth of fuel on the way to the appointment.

Pat also divulged that he had never hung around talking with the top sales performers in the organisation. Other winners are the best ones to hang out with in the sales industry. Just one tip or suggestion can make a significant difference to your success. All the little things help. Remember large doors swing open on tiny hinges!

Pat should consider new ways to:

❖ Show confidence by stating his business right up front.

113

❖ State why he is there and what he will be doing.

❖ Get early agreement that the prospect understands the process and there will be no unpleasant surprises.

Chapter 22. **Help Them To Help You:** Ask the right questions.

To me, asking the right questions is overrated. I never try to make out that I know everything about the industry or the job of the prospect that I have the good fortune to be visiting. As everyone believes that their circumstances are unique and special, and they are, I never want to look as though I know more about their industry, or their lives, than they do. I would much rather give the impression that I am a little naïve or uninformed but eager to learn.

That way I gain a lot more information because they will go a lot further into their explanation of their industry, or their job. I ask these conditioning questions as a guide to get them relaxing and opening up, and connecting with me. For this to happen the questions all need to be open ended to get the conversation going, and information flowing.

Later on in the meeting I will switch to more uncomfortable, invasive, closed questions that require very specific answers, or rhetorical questions that only require 'Yes' or 'No' as an answer, which stop any discussion. All good defence lawyers know this. Imagine if they asked an overly intense closed question first. Consider the scenario, "Did you kill him?", 'Yes.' – 'Guilty,' case closed.

You want the conversation to flow in the early stages, so ask comfortable, non- invasive, non-intimidating, questions that encourage, as opposed to halting conversation and discussion. We all know these words, they are our old friends 'who, what, when, where, why and how'. These words feature in nearly every sales book and sales manual ever written. It is amazing that some salespeople have forgotten how, and when to use them in the initial interview stage of identifying and analysing the prospects needs. It is in the early stages when you must draw them out in a discussion to identify the need for your service or product. Even if they have told you what they need at the outset, your job is to gather information and delve further, to help and guide them in maximising your opportunity to serve them well.

"The customer pays your wages." - Henry Ford.

Your needs-identifying discovery questions must bring all of their, yet unexpressed and maybe unrealised needs out on the table. This is where 'Lead Quality' comes in, because you can now rank and weigh the prospects needs based upon the answers to these questions you are about to ask. This methodology must be standardised for best practices across your whole organisation. As a result, your questions will become like heat-seeking missiles as opposed to scattered machine gun fire.

The only effective way at this point is to ask a few well thought-out questions to uncover what is important to the prospect, so structure your questions with those thoughts in mind. The questions must be open-ended. Your aim is to uncover needs and wants in a way that gives you the best possible chance to design that solution. For that to happen you must first get yourself firmly into the prospects mind and also walk a mile in their shoes, so that your solution produces an outcome that will mean you become an important part of their business or life. Every sales situation is different, so to formulate your own questions I suggest you start by asking yourself questions such as:

- How will my customers' lives be better because of them dealing with me and using my product or service?

- How will by using me, make them feel and act for the better?

- What are the most likely positive feelings they will gain?

- How will our proposal add serious value to this prospects life and or business?

- Who else needs to be involved?

- What level of service do they require?

- What level of service can they afford?

- What will be the consequences to them if they do not proceed with our product or service and solution?

- What is their timing going to be?

- How do we best connect with them?

- How are they currently missing out on profit that we could alter?

- In the event that we can't help them who can we refer them to who can?

Asking questions is possibly the only time when you leave modern technology in your bag. At the first appointment meeting get out your best pen and a blank piece of writing paper, ask permission to take notes and then write the words "Strictly Confidential" in large letters across the top of that paper. Focus on listening to what the prospective client has to say in their reply. Keep control of the process by keeping it on track using questions. When the prospects answers are delivered too quickly you keep control by simply asking them to slow down a little bit. You are not manipulating the client but simply keeping control so that the best outcome can be achieved for both parties as quickly and conveniently as possible. When people see that you are writing down their answers they also tend to stick fairly close to the truth. Exaggeration is dropped, which means your solution should then be accurate.

Don't just listen really listen. You can tell when you are in the presence of a good listener; they are a joy to be around. Great listeners never let accents, biases, emotion, personal looks, hairstyles, dress, religious beliefs, gender, skin colour, age, speech volume, speed of speaking, dryness of delivery, or other matters distract them or throw them off the task. They just focus on the message.

You can build a checklist of your own questions to cover with your prospective clients or customers in any given circumstance without leading, prompting or interrupting. Here are a few examples:

- Why have you decided to explore this avenue?

- What do you expect your requirements will be for …?

- What process did you go through to determine your needs?

- Where do you see this happening?

- When do you see the potential benefits happening?

- When have you had the most success in the past?

- With who have you had difficulties in the past?

- Can you put that another way to help me understand it a little better?

- What does that mean?

- Which process is still working best for you now?

- What challenges do those matters create?

- Why has that created such a problem in the past?

- What are the best things about that system?

- How many other issues in relation to that concern would you like to discuss?

- What do you like most about…?"

- What aspect of your current arrangements would you like improved the most?"

Whenever they express something that they see as a big issue then you should refer to them as 'problems'. However, when you want to take the weight off that issue you should then refer to those matters as "concerns". I don't know about you, but selling is hard enough without making it even more difficult by discussing problems that your solution can't fix. Never assume you know how they are going to answer.

Ask your question and wait patiently for the answer. Even if you have been in the industry for ten years or longer and think you've heard it all, don't make the mistake of assuming you know what the prospect's needs are. Let them tell you, rather than your telling them. People will tell you everything you want to know. All you need to do is ask. Most people love to talk about themselves and want to share information about their current situation, their challenges or problems, likes and dislikes. It amazes me how few salespeople actually take the time to learn about their clients and customers before they launch into their presentation.

Focus on how the prospect can eventually benefit the most from your proposal.

The person asking the questions and holding the pen is quietly in control. People who have done my training program learn about a very simple mental picture of a segmented cog that I keep in my head so that I know at all times where I am in the sales process COG as shown in Diagram 'A'. The cog gives me a very clearly structured, formal, presentation so that I know where I am at any given time. It really helps in getting to yes! Yes, I know that sales teams are equipped with generic printed material and glossy booklets but ask yourself how customised does that look to a prospective customer. To me it's a matter of mass produced versus hand crafted. (For corporate clients with specialised equipment you can substitute pen and paper with high tech iPad's and electronic computerised whiteboards if they are in regular use there). Think about the last time you visited a top solicitor, or a top accountant.

Firstly, how much were they charging you an hour and secondly what was the next thing they did? My bet is the top ones would have taken out a lined blank pad of grey paper with their logo at the top, thus creating the impression that they have no preconceived opinion or idea on what your problem is. Any printed material is always available to be handed out if the client requires it. In reality, they have probably handled the same problem many times.

They simply duck out to the back of their office and have a paralegal person or someone on a far lower hourly rate use a template, and bang out the solution and then charge you several hundred dollars an hour for several hours' service. You pay top dollars because you perceive them as the solution to your legal matters and you feel you have received good value from them if the outcome is good. The same as any top salesperson will do with a proposal or planned solution for their client. Salespeople have to put the same, if not more value on their time than other professionals do.

Therefore, the questions we ask must be to the point and directly related to your product or service. Unless you are selling weather vanes, there is no sense in asking them about the weather. If I am selling to a business or corporation then I would say something along these lines:

Obviously, I use their name but only after, I have checked with them how they would like me to address them. There is nothing that sounds worse than a salesperson meeting a prospect named Denise, then two minutes later be calling her Den as they often do with my sister Denise.

> *"We would like to understand how your business runs and then how our solution can impact on your profitability. Would you mind if I ask you some questions so that I can carry out a discovery schedule (or needs analysis) on your business operation and your company model? We think we can improve your sales but we need to understand your situation before we present any solution to you. Is that okay?"*

Now, please picture for a moment two people holding a conversation and ask yourself which of these people believes what they are saying is true. The answer is both of them believe what they are saying is true. That doesn't necessarily mean that they believe what the other person is saying is necessarily true. So now we have established that they believe what they are saying is true why not let them say it?

At this point of the sales COG, we are doing a guided discovery, obviously with the intent of isolating the problems and finding out how our solution will help. It is an in-depth process so if you have used the old standard J. Douglas Edwards technique, and adopted by many others, of asking them for 15 minutes of their time, unless you have questions then at this point you will be in big trouble.

Be assured that top business people love seeing top salespeople in action, it is better than the opera or a good show for them. As a peak performer I want them thinking wow what do I have to do to get this guy on my team to sell for me. Only poor sales performers would ask for 15 minutes and then push for more so why not be honest up front and say "For us to do a proper job for you we require an hour or so of your time. We consider our time valuable and we certainly respect that your time is valuable also so we promise not to waste either. Is that okay?"

Notice that I tie down as often as I can with a rhetorical question that requires a yes or no answer. I then go on to say things like:

"Please be assured that if during our discovery
schedule process we find that we can't help you we
would like to be the first to tell you. Is that all right?
But on the other hand if we do discover that our
solution can help you, we would like to come back
with an in-depth proposal to present to you and all
the other decision-makers involved in saying yes to
our proposal. Are you happy with that?"

Then I revert to general open-ended questions that require a good detailed open answer. Starting with gentler warming up questions, I then gradually progress to more in-depth ones. Most salespeople who I have observed have a reasonably good handle on who, what, why and how questions. The massive mistake that they make is then to jump from what the prospect has told them straight to a demonstration of their own product or service. Seeing Salespeople do this makes me hum the words to Meat Loaf's famous song:

"Paradise by the dashboard light"

Ain't no doubt about it
We were doubly blessed
Cause we were barely seventeen
And we were barely dressed

Ok, here we go, we got a real pressure cooker
going here, two down, nobody on, no score,
bottom of the ninth, there's the wind-up and
there it is, a line shot up the middle, look
at him go. This boy can really fly!

He's rounding first and really turning it on
now, he's not letting up at all, he's gonna
try for second; the ball is bobbled out in centre,
and here comes the throw, and what a throw!
He's gonna slide in head first, here he comes, he's out!

No, wait, safe—safe at second base, this kid really makes
things happen out there.
Batter steps up to the plate, here's the pitch--
he's going, and what a jump he's got, he's trying for third,
here's the throw, it's in the dirt--
safe at third! Holy cow, stolen base!
He's taking a pretty big lead out there, almost
daring him to try and pick him off.

We all know what happened next, when he attempted home base too soon.

In selling, there are specialists who have expertise from having done their trade or years of university or whatever, and then there are those with a more general background. From a logistics perspective, if you discover that the prospect requires very technical aspects for their business solution that you can't cover, knowing this is very important for selling; you invite an expert in to help. As the provider of the solution, your role is to either have a very in-depth knowledge of the customers business or refer to an expert. Experts can answer the customers question in detail based on evidence, experience, and facts. The generalist on the other hand, when caught in a technical situation, must ask permission to defer to expertise and get back to them.

What habits must Pat improve, to go from mediocre to champion?

Pat was excessively presumptuous. He asked them questions and let them speak but went ahead far too quickly. He gave the impression that he already knew the answer and just wanted to blurt that answer out. Pat should consider new ways to:

- ❖ Use questions as a guide.
- ❖ Make a real effort and listen first.
- ❖ Keep control by use of questions.

Chapter 23. **<u>Prospects Always Want To Know:</u>** What's in it for me?

Whenever you meet someone in a sales environment, please keep in mind that in their reasoning eventually, they have got the old question coined in the acronym 'WIIFM', or to spell it out fully the expression is "What's in it for me?" (Alternatively, "What's in it for us?" If it is a business or corporation). Knowing that this is always in their mind, helps you keep your thoughts very clear, and yourself singularly focused in the present moment. COG that I use means that you do not race ahead because you can alter the pace. It ensures that you stay intently focused on the prospect, their needs, and how you can provide them with the perfect solution.

The first few minutes of the meeting are where you use your elevator statement. An elevator statement is just a brief statement that you have which is a remarkably clear and concise description of what you do. So when anyone asks you what you do, you can tell them clearly in a very short period of time. Like the time you would have available in an elevator ride.

This description of you and your product and service should be a concise, benefit-laden, and accurate summary of what you do in order for it to have a direct and sufficiently powerful impact so that you will be top of mind when the need arises.

Be ready for them to stop you there and then to ask for your card. That's your opportunity to make an appointment. Your elevator statement must sell, the crunch not the apple, the sizzle not the steak! You should consider your elevator statement carefully so that it answers reasonable questions in the customers mind even before they ask them.

Questions such as:

Exactly what is it that you do?

How do you do it better than any other company does?

Why should any customer buy from you rather than your opposition?

What would your competition say that your company does better than anyone else does?

What would your satisfied existing customers say that your company does better than any other company?

Your goal is to have your elevator statement describe what is unique about your company's approach. This is your 'USP,' which stands for 'Unique Selling Proposition'. As you work through COG, you can then match those characteristics more closely to the expectations of potential customers. Our elevator statement is:

"We provide a customised professional sales system that is easy for everyone who is communicating with the customer to understand and use. Using that system we take our client company's sales results from where they are to where they want to be.'

What habits must Pat improve, to go from mediocre to champion?

When Pat told them that he had been a schoolteacher I would have preferred to hear him say something like, "Now, I help people just like you create wealth for themselves so that they can live worry free knowing that their future is very well catered for." Then, I think that those prospects would have been all ears.

Pat should consider new ways to:

❖ Become more customer focused.

❖ Think through their answers.

❖ Ask for clarification on any points he does not clearly understand.

Chapter 24. **<u>Desire Before Demonstration:</u>** Intensify the need first.

At this point, you have built rapport and have asked the right questions to qualify your prospect. This was discussed in the first of the eight segments in the Professional Sales COG. You then progressed to capturing their interest, and discovered if they had any need for your product or service. As soon as a need was identified, a mediocre salesperson would have dived straight into the show and tell. Smarter operators know that you never move to the 'Dog and Pony' show stage before you have intensified the need. This is also known as, 'the disturb'. Unless you disturb, you do not create desire. Unless you create desire, you do not make a sale.

A desire to buy requires your prospect to have a real need for your offer, and to know what you are talking about. You need to spend a short time intensifying the need and creating a burning desire for your solution. If what you are offering is the wrong product or service, or the prospect is the wrong person, politely end the conversation right there. Say this isn't the case, continue by restating the needs that the prospect has identified, and written down in a list.

Ask them to prioritise those needs and offer to discard any they can easily remedy by themselves. Ask the prospect, with the exception of money, to list and then rate these needs from one to ten, in order of importance. Note these priorities down, verbatim for inclusion in your solution proposal. Nearly all, but the best salespeople, miss out this essential step. I have never been exactly sure why, they might just like the sound of their own voices.

Maybe they prefer to take what they see as the easy way out, and jump straight to the demonstration stage in which they are more comfortable. Perhaps sheer enthusiasm overcomes them. More than likely they have simply never been shown how to do it properly.

To help you understand the GOG stages better, an analogy is useful. Picture a high, snow covered mountain. This mountain will represent the sale as a whole. Now imagine that you the salesperson has to climb, with your prospect, up and over that mountain to complete the sales process. Let us say the prospect in this case is a man.

Your route must take you up one side and right over the top of the peak, then down the other side to the concluded sale. You have only limited supplies, and there are time constraints. The weather forecast predicts fog is approaching; this represents the prospects uncertainties and something, which if not kept ahead of will see them turn back. Time is of the essence.

The initial slope is everything you have done up to and including the discovery schedule. You finished writing down the answers to the questions you have asked, and these have been prioritised. The first side of the mountain rises gently at first but increases rapidly. It is far and away the hardest side to climb. There are obstacles; snow, trees, and rocks are the prospects questions through which you must negotiate.

You are now getting near the peak of the first slope. You must climb right over the peak to go down the other side, taking short cuts disqualifies you. Effectively you have planned the climb, bought the maps and all the mountaineering equipment; the suit, the car, a smart briefcase, the lead, and everything you need for the appointment.

You ascend slowly being careful, and watching your every move. You are almost at the peak, when your companion, the prospect, suddenly slows down. He cannot see the value of the journey. He has had enough, and his enthusiasm for this climb is starting to wane. The second thoughts that he may have, might cause the prospect to stop right here, and turn around and leave. Carrying him on your shoulders is not an option because he is too heavy. Similarly, you rule out dragging him because you are not strong enough and need to conserve your energy.

130

Despite the prospects hesitation, you just want to get over the top and down the other side to the close. The down slope, on the other side of the mountain is the home stretch that is much easier, it is downhill. This homeward slope is where you show and tell. Demonstrate and then handle objections as you go. The very bottom of that slope is where it becomes sympathetic and gentle; this is the final close.

To go further you now need to inspire the prospect, and give him a reason to stick with you for the rest of the journey across the peak. This may involve telling him an account of a client in a similar position. You stand near him, and both look back down the mountain. Let him see the potential hazards for himself, the time wasted and a chance of missing out on your solution. Let him point these hazards out to you; resist the temptation to point them out to him. Perhaps he see's the dark clouds looming, and the wind that has whipped up through the valley behind you.

Let him decide for himself that the trip back does not look the safer option anymore. You ask him to cast his eyes around the sides of the mountain. You can see low-lying fog, so skirting around the peak is too difficult and will take too long. Crossing over the peak is the only way. Ask the prospect to confirm that staying still or going back is not an option. Remind him of the dangers. Now, you point out the good news, the clear skies ahead, and the easy slide down the gentler side to the close. Which direction do you think that he will choose to take? As you start towards the top again, ask the right questions and he will say let's cross the peak. These questions are no longer general ones they are qualifying ones. They relate to your list of priorities, only this time they are probing questions that require specific answers. Questions like:

- If we can find a solution, who are the people who will need to be involved?

- What action steps will need to be taken?

- What is your timeline for implementing?

- What other matters should we be made aware of before moving forward?

- What are your thoughts?

- What could change?

- What concerns do you have?

- How do you measure that?

In other words, you have now both progressed to within a short distance from the peak. Suddenly, you both pause and look at each other. Right near the summit, you discover a chasm. This crack in the mountain is deep with jagged sharp rocks, and you cannot see the bottom of it. Metaphorically, the 'buy-line' is right in the centre of the chasm. The chasm represents the salespersons difficulty in helping the prospect over the buy-line. You have to cross this chasm before you can progress to demonstrating your solution. The problem is that the gap is always just marginally wider than anyone can jump. Falling in would mean no sale. Hesitate here and the sale is stranded in no-man's land. The prospect will thank you for your time and back out.

At this juncture, an average salesperson would get to the chasm and then go 'to heck with it', grab the prospect, summon up all their strength and take a mighty leap of faith. Salespeople like this will get to the end of the questions and say something like:

'Thanks for taking the time and answering all my questions. Now, let me show you how we can help you."

Using this approach, the salesperson is still selling and the prospect considers, or feels, that they are being sold something. Remember how people dislike being sold to. Do you ever arrive home with something new and proclaim. 'Look what someone has just sold me". You don't do you? So how do we get the prospect over the chasm, (over the buy-line) to become a willing buyer and an advocate of your product or service?

Back to the mountain analogy; remember where you and the prospect are at the precipice. You have prepared, struggled and clambered nearly to the top of the first side, and then you are hit with a deep ravine that is full of potential catastrophes. These are known as objections. You must overcome these fear-packed, 'rejection producers' to get over the chasm to safety.

How can you possibly get both of you across safely to get home to a concluded sale? Think hard.

That's right. To cross this exceedingly dangerous ravine safely to get to the side of the slope, where they are buying you must first build a bridge. Figuratively, work together to find a fallen tree, or two, long enough to lie across the gap and build a bridge. In other words, make them feel safe in crossing with you, from the 'being sold to' side of the chasm to the 'wanting to buy' side. To get them to step onto the bridge means that they will have strengthened their own belief in your ability to provide the ideal solution for their needs and wants.

Master this step, and you have mastered the art of selling!

The secret lies in crossing the bridge with confidence knowing that all the way down the downward slope they are buying from you. You are no longer selling to them. So the questions we need to ask now are deeply probing questions that require one word answers. They have the two objectives in mind in this order; Importance and Urgency. That is called, 'disturbing' or intensifying the need. The questions are:

1) "How important is it, that you solve them?

2) "When do you need to have these solutions solved?

(Any other answer and you slip back down the slope and start again with more qualifying questions.) The answers you are seeking sound like, 'Very' and 'extremely,' and 'Now.' They will finally say something such as, "Tell me Phil, how we can get hold of this?" That's Gold! That is exactly what you are looking for and you know that they have now stepped onto the bridge with you.

But wait, there is one more concern. The bridge must be strong so they feel comfortable crossing it with you. Here, is how you do that, it's known as 'determining value and tying down'. It involves asking the prospect to put a dollar value on the solution that they want.

But, hang on a minute. Why am I giving you this absolute gem that will boost your sales through the roof? Well you are reading my book, so I have probably already identified a need that you have, and I assume that you are interested in improving your sales results and, therefore, your income. Firstly, let me ask you the two vital value-establishing questions:

1. 'How important is it that you boost your sales even by 20%'?

2. 'When is the best time to do that? '

I hope that your answers to those questions are, "it is very important that I boost sales: and 'Now' is the best time." Then, moving forward to my third value-establishing question, where I want you to give me an exact answer expressed as a total monetary sum.

Therefore, the next question is, covered in the next chapter.

What habits must Pat improve, to go from mediocre to champion?

Without intensifying the need and creating desire, you have no sale. The person standing in the rain, with holes in the soles of their only pair of shoes understands this. They just want to find the nearest shoe shop and buy another pair. They are over that buy-line before they enter the store. Pat is like the vast majority of salespeople who never take the vital few seconds to add the intensifying the need questions to his presentation and then tie down.

Pat should consider new ways to:

❖ Get across the 'buy-line' because simply taking a leap of faith is usually disastrous.

❖ Learn how to build that bridge and help them over it safely.

❖ Wind back to an earlier point in the COG until the need is intensified.

Chapter 25. **The Hunted Becomes the Hunter:** When they cross the 'buy-line.'

We are on the bridge now only one tiny step away from the 'buy-line'. The next step is known as tying down, so please follow carefully as we nurse each other over that line.

My first two value establishing questions hopefully have you crossing the bridge with me. In other words, you are now just one tiny step away from the 'buy-line. Those questions were:

1. 'How important is it that you boost your sales even by 20%?'

2. 'When is the best time to do that? '

Your answers to those questions hopefully were, "it is very important that I boost sales": and "Now" is the best time."

My aim with the third 'value establishing' question is to get you to give me an exact answer expressed as a total monetary sum. Therefore, my third question to you, dear prospect would be:

3. In the next 12 months, how much money will that mean to your bottom-line?

Let's say you answer; 'I will make an extra $20,000 over the next 12 months'. My response will be "so, if I show you my solution, that will make you $20,000 or more over the next twelve months that means $200,000, or more, over the next ten years doesn't it? The answer is a 'no-brainer' 'Yes'. Bear with me as I now want to tie you down (it is only a figure of speech) and have you fully committed to using my solution. Therefore, my next question is a rhetorical one. A rhetorical question is a statement that requires no answer. It literally answers itself. So, I will say to you something that ties our discussions tightly together. For example, "The property you can buy with that extra $200,000 is what you really want, isn't it?

Now provided you are nodding at me, and once I have heard you utter these precise answers you have made statements to me that I can pretty much guess that the next words out of your mouth are going to be: "Phil, please tell me what I have to do to make more sales?" Bingo-you are now buying my solution, and I am no longer selling to you. We are both over the 'buy-line' off the bridge and on the easy slope to home. You have conquered the mountain.

From here, I now want to switch to handling your objections, providing details and demonstrating to you, what you need to do next. You can see how powerful that is can't you? I need to summarise what has happened in specific chunks, so you can clearly see step by step what I have just done. Obviously if, you do not answer; 'Very Important', and 'Now' and provide me with a specific dollar value then I will know that I have not built the bridge successfully. When that occurs I will go back to asking further 'needs identifying' questions.

What I have done is listen carefully to your needs. I've written them down using your words, I've asked you to prioritise those needs; this is where most average salespeople jump in and enthusiastically tells the client what they can do for them. Now I've intensified the need in your mind by specifically asking you how important it is that you find a solution.

You observe that I am no longer asking you questions that require an open-ended answer. I am now asking you questions that require a very specific answer. This is exactly what I do with clients. If you miss this stage, you miss a great percentage of sales that you otherwise should have made and, therefore, missed the opportunity to put a greater amount of money into your bank account.

Now I don't know about you, but I imagine if I went to the local supermarket and asked if I could pay for my grocery bill on potential future sales that they would laugh me out the door. The only thing they want is my cash. Hence, I know as a salesperson that I need to do my job well in order to keep my life running as comfortably as I like. Helping my clients to prosper is always my priority.

Then because I know that all objections come down to five basic ones, I want the answer to be specific. To cover 'need', I asked you how important is it that you boost sales, say even by 20% and you answered 'very'. Then secondly, I asked you "when is the best time to do that?" In other words when is the best time to boost your sales and you answered "now," so I've covered the basic objection of 'hurry'.

Then I asked you what would this mean to you in terms of money in your pocket over the next 12 months and you answered with a specific dollar amount that was large enough to be specific and way larger than the asking price for my book of $29.95.

In fact, the figure of $20,000 would mean you are getting better than a 50,000% return on investment. Over a ten-year period, multiply that by 10. That covers the basic objection of 'money'. By the way, if I didn't believe I could make you any extra money by using my professional sales system then I would tell you. I would bring that figure back to a smaller more palatable amount. Even if you only make $2,000 dollars, in the next 12 months, that will still be $20,000 over the next 10 years. I am sure you would still see that my $29.95 as being great value for money.

Now, if I did not believe that I would not tell you, so I have now covered the next basic objection of belief. Almost, but in this day and age of scepticism and instant Google I know without asking that you will still want to see the evidence and that's what I'll show you in the proposal presentation stage. Had I been asking $20,000 for my book then to make you $20,000 would not be appealing because you would obviously have gained no financial benefit from your investment.

Now, I know there is only one basic objection left the one of 'trust'! Before this meeting is over you are going to receive some objections. If you haven't then please, prompt some by saying, 'Now here's something you may be worried about.' Or, 'The last client who went ahead with us was originally worried about…' Anything that gets them putting up an objection.

What habits must Pat improve, to go from mediocre to champion?

Pat relied on his PowerPoint presentation for the disturb, he showed no empathy with the clients concerns.

Pat should consider new ways to:

❖ Get to grips with the correct way to create desire.

❖ Never rush past until the buy-line is crossed.

❖ Lead the prospect logically to a buying decision.

Chapter 26. **Pre-empting Objections:** Beat them to the punch.

Objections! Top sales performers love them, average sales performers fear them, and dud salespeople hate them. Amateur salespeople just ploy on past them, hoping that more talking will mean they will go away. The fact is you can never get to 'Yes' without them, so learn to embrace and love objections. It is my firm belief that you should work as hard as you can in your precious face-to-face time with the prospect, or ear-to-ear time on the telephone, to get out as many of their objections as you possibly can no matter how minor they may appear.

No objection is too small; as you are going through all discussions keep digging for their objections in order to manage them as you go. It is impossible for me to list all the objections you can get because your product would be quite different from mine, but let me tell you that whilst there are many objections and no doubt, you have heard them, they all fall into only five major categories.

That's right. As hard as it might be for you to believe, there are only five major categories of objections and they are:-

1. No Trust or Belief.

2. No Need.

3. No Desire.

4. No Hurry and Importance.

5. No Money.

The first rule, in COG, of handling any objection is to welcome it. Use a statement something like, "That's a good question and I'm glad that you have bought it up." In the few split seconds, it takes you to say that, you should have thought of the answer. The human mind can think six or seven times faster than humans usually speak. Usual speaking speed is about one-hundred and ten words a minute, so thinking speed is more than seven-hundred words a minute. While you are welcoming, that gives you plenty of thinking time to come up with a reason why you are so glad. Welcoming an objection is one thing, but a thorough understanding of how to handle them is another.

The idea of getting every objection out is to allow you to disarm them and tie down on them as you go. There are sometimes situations where objections can not be answered. These are in fact not objections; they are 'conditions'. Conditions are true statements, not easily identified in pre-qualifying, that describe circumstances that are impossible to overcome. Some examples might be; prospects permanent ill health, potential loss of job, or issues of poor credit.

Let's now build your sales armoury, for handling objections. Start with a good collection of authentic anecdotes: actual events that have happened either in your own life or one of your client's lives. The stories are often what the client will remember most about you. Stories are the essence of persuasive communication, provided the listener believes them. They can take the listener on an emotional ride, in any colour they want.

Hollywood was built on storytelling. The art is in the telling. Lame and boring puts people to sleep, so zip and vitality are the keys. I still have people coming up to me, many years after I first met them and reminding me of one story, or another that I told them. You could outline a memorable event or situation, which ties in to a satisfied customer.

Prior to meeting you, that now satisfied customer might have had the same or similar set of problems that the prospect sitting with you now has. Paint the picture so that the prospects see themselves in that picture as though they have already had the benefit of your solution. In 1993, I stayed with my friends Herschel Gordon Lewis and his lovely wife Margo at their fabulous home in Plantation, Florida. I believe Herschel to be one of the greatest writers of direct mail copy ever.

Brad Antin, from Kansas, is another. Whilst there, he introduced me to the word 'verisimilitude', which is a noun meaning, 1) the appearance, or semblance of truth; likelihood; probability: 2). something, as an assertion, having the appearance of truth. Herschel taught me to never tell a story that lacks verisimilitude. Your story should be the gospel truth. Even then, it may still sound untrue. Test your stories for verisimilitude (it's the only big word that I've used) with someone you trust. Ask them for a reaction and you will know how to tell them a better way.

Once you have grasped the concept of all objections falling into only five major categories, you can tell a story related to that objection. Tell it in a light-hearted way, using strong active language that brings it to life, before the objection actually comes up. The prospect, then feels that you have lifted the weight off that objection. This is reassuring for them because they know that you are not afraid of their objection. Once you have lifted the weight then you must tie down with a rhetorical question that requires a 'Yes' or, 'No' response. "So we can handle that for you then. That will make you happy won't it?"

Use your training sessions to fire objections backwards and forwards to each other. Politicians do the same. They sit out the back with the spin doctors firing questions at them in simulated interviews. Then when the real discussion takes place on the television or in the newspapers they don't look extremely stupid. After all, they are salespeople. If they do not sell the policies, then they don't get the votes. That is why they employ so many spin-doctors.

Handle the objections one at a time with the intention of not only finally getting to "Yes" but also defying them to say, "No." Then, your close is almost assured.

Procrastination fits somewhere between objection and condition. It needs to be addressed because it can instantly kill deals. Procrastinators will usually only act once it's too late. A good example is middle men who don't care much about their health and fitness until after their first heart attack.

A good way to handle procrastination is to use the 'feel, felt, found' technique. Where you tell a story by saying, "I know exactly how you feel, I have another client who felt the same way and here is what they found." The story that you relate then ties in with the urgency and desire becoming greater than the fears driving the procrastination.

Let's now handle each major objection one at a time:

No Trust or belief.

Provided your prospect has the financial resources, then the trust objection will be the biggest objection of all. This objection is rarely disclosed to you because people do not often want to show they don't trust you. That is tantamount to calling you a liar. Using 'liar' is something that people as human beings tend to avoid especially if they are not sure how you will react. It is always the colossal elephant in the room. Think about the last person that you met that for some reason, you distrusted. Was it the look of their eyes, was it the way they smelled, was it how they shook your hand? And so on. There are many reasons why they may not trust you, only you can work on this. Trust differs from belief - let me explain. Someone who you trust may still say something that you don't believe. Likewise, someone who you do not trust may still say something that you believe.

If the first impression, you have made on your prospect has been a good one (you only ever have one chance to make a first impression):

- ❖ You have spent time building rapport.

- ❖ Your testimonials stack up, your company is honourable.

- ❖ They like your enthusiasm and approach.

- ❖ You were on time.

❖ You've looked them in the eye and shaken hands properly, listened carefully.

❖ You've taken meticulous notes, and you've done all the intangible things we have spoken about.

Right there, you have already gone a long way towards building their confidence, especially if they are a referral lead. The body language experts tell us that, in part, you can gain people's trust by mirroring them. Watch any two people at a bar and if, in effect, they are getting on well, they will be standing and acting in a mirror image. I think that the easier way to build trust is to show proof of what you're saying, for example, photographs, testimonials or recognised expert opinion. Maybe, show an article from a respected newspaper or magazine.

The timing of your reply to any objection is also crucial to build trust. When a prospective client throws, you an objection, and you respond with a rapid-fire answer then you will look as if you haven't thought it through and the client may well distrust your response. Contrary to that if you take too long to respond then they will think you either, don't know the answer, or that they have trapped you. So the timing of your answer is important. Just hold your tongue for one or two seconds. Although you know the answer, have practised it repeatedly, and it's on the tip of your tongue, just hold off for a second or two.

Not too long. The client may also doubt you if you look as if you're stumped on their question, and then you've stabbed a guess or made-up an answer that you really just plucked out of nowhere. To me it is better, to let them know that you don't know the answer, but with one phone call to your team you can find out. For example, I would say, "I don't know the answer to that, but if it is really essential to you then I can make a phone call right now and get you the answer. Is that Okay?

Clients may also distrust you if you look away or start fidgeting when you give an answer. Video yourself during a real live sales appointment, then you can see what you actually do when working under that pressure. You will be surprised. Once you've seen the faults then work hard to resolve them. COG is all about strengthening your strengths and eliminating your weaknesses.

Clients may also distrust you if they discover that you also do work for, or provide product to someone who they deem to be the opposition, and fear their opposition is being informed by you. Often in business, you are supplying the same industry, and it's only natural for people to push you for information about their opposition.

The truck driver in your organisation may be telling the forklift driver in the opposition's business information they shouldn't be. It is called bragging, and gossip and takes no account of true and false. People love a juicy bit of gossip, especially if they feel that the truth is being deliberately withheld from them. They will often make up gossip rather than admit they don't know. It's hard to stop but work on it please, because gossip travels. Once it reaches the ears of your potential customer, no matter what you say, that objection is almost impossible to overcome if they believe that gossip coming from your organisation will damage their own profit.

"A lie gets halfway around the world before the truth has a chance to get its pants on." - Winston Churchill (1874-1965).

On the subject, of truck drivers, they may also distrust your business if a truck, a delivery van, or a company car with your logo all over the side has cut across their lane on that morning, or double-parked beside them somewhere. The moral of that story is if you have a truck driver then, please don't force them to rush. Rushed drivers can damage your company's image, and trust with the client beyond belief.

Frequently, it's not the truck driver's fault; it's the truck dispatcher's manager's fault if they are pushing them to unrealistic deadlines. It's also worth remembering that no matter how smart you are you can never stop everyone from talking. Similarly, if, you have told a particular client one thing about delivery, and then another person from your organisation gives another answer then trust is broken.

A recent example that I saw in a freight company involved a general salesperson who had the title Business Development Manager on his business card. When he was, asked a specific question about what type of trailer was needed to move a large compressor unit he answered "I'll have to check with Head Office for you and come back to you as soon as I can". The generalist had two options he could either guess or revert. He could tell them that he did not know but could find out. Alternatively, he could take a wild stab and guess. Checking and reverting is a strategy when not knowing an answer.

If you don't know what you are talking about then record or remember the question, consult with your expert and come back to the customer. Ask the prospect how serious getting the answer to their technical question really is. That client may have just been using the technical question to check if you were being honest about your level of knowledge. The answer may not be necessary at all. Best to admit when you don't know the answer.

Belief and trust go hand in hand, yet they differ slightly. The truth isn't accepted as being the truth until people believe you. Those with the ability to drill right down into the human psyche would probably tell you that the thing anyone in business fears the most is being made to look a fool in the eyes of their peers. They may be fully praying for your solution to fix their problems. Unless they simply do not believe you, then they will not proceed simply out of fear of looking foolish, even if they desperately want to believe you, which after all is your intention. They will most likely still need proof of what you can do.

Seeing is believing!

People won't believe you if they can't understand what you are saying, and they won't know what you're saying if they don't listen to you. They won't listen to you if you're not engaging, and you won't be compelling until you say things in an original, captivating and innovative way. Remember this is the "no bullshit selling" way. The adage 'if it sounds too good to be true don't do it' applies more now than when it was first used. So you should make sure that your submission never sounds too good to be true because it will not be believed. Even if it is true! The truth isn't altered by how many people believe you, but verisimilitude may affect that.

Sensational claims about your product or service may be difficult for the prospect to swallow more than once or twice. Your testimonials therefore, will need to act as proof of your claims by way of a third person endorsement. Let the endorser use their own words in a testimonial. You will be surprised just how admirable people will be, provided you have genuinely been the answer to their problem whatever your field is. The more dramatic, the result has been in these real-life battlefield success stories that you have created for your clients the better. Remember it is someone else endorsing you and that is a powerful form of selling.

In sales, it is reasonable to assume that at the level you are dealing with, all of your customers have a good understanding of their own industry. Therefore, a salesperson or a Business Development Manager is expected to equal or exceed that understanding of expertise. A Business Development Manager who fails to do this doesn't make sales because they lack creditability in the eyes of the customer. What effect does this have?

The lack of knowledge means that: someone can't describe a palatable solution to a customer. They can't explain how their own company's product or service is going to solve the customer's problems because they can't explain what the customers problems are in the proper way. Let alone what is proposed as the recommended solution.

By the way, let me stress again that if you don't have a strong belief in yourself and your own abilities to successfully handle any issues that any customer throws at you and your company's product and services, no matter what you say, the customer will struggle to believe you. It's a subconscious thing. Here, is as good a time as any to stress that. So believe in yourself, and your service, or get out of selling.

"You become what you believe." – Oprah Winfrey.

No Needs and Wants.

Simply stated a need is something you have to have, while a want is something you would like to have. The most basic 'needs' are oxygen, water, food, clothing and shelter. Beyond those are 'wants'. Many things can meet your basic needs. A tent for shelter, a blanket for clothing, rainwater for water and some bread are all that is needed for basic survival. Wants have nothing to do with basic survival. What do we want?

In business, we want to stay ahead of the competition, we want to be more effective, we want to grow, and we want to make more money. In our personal lives, we want better houses, better cars, great relationships, more money and so on. We want to acquire and accumulate. A little is good, but more is better.

Even if right now a company has enough money it will always want to make more. It's called the bottom-line, and that is the nature of democracy and commerce. People are the same in their own lives. They all want to make more money. I am yet to meet a millionaire who doesn't want to make another million. However, what do they gain from more money? How about higher net worth, increased intrinsic value, higher, greater profit margin, share value, financial security. Alternatively, perhaps a secure retirement or their child's future college tuition paid for, or their student loans paid off. Therefore, once we have identified needs we need to show them as 'wants' to attract and stimulate the desire factor. Once again, it's the crunch, not the apple scenario. The sizzle not the steak as Don Beveridge always said.

An insurance company representative, whose company we trained, once came into my office and told me that he was going to be the next successful sales trainer, bigger than Ben Hur in his own mind. Another person in our office was a talented salesperson and trainer and, on hearing, this offered a challenge to the insurance guy. The challenge was that the insurance company representative would give our man two of his hardest leads that he had yet to settle, and then they would both follow those two leads diligently, and by the following Friday would report to the sales meeting. At the sales meeting, it was decided to phone the two leads and put them on the loud speaker phone.

So, in front of some 30 or so high achieving ego-driven insurance salespeople, (now more regulated, up skilled and formally qualified as financial planners) we heard the only lead who they could get hold of answer the question; which of the two salespeople was the best? The lead answered that the insurance salesperson had been by far the best; he had a printed compendium he had high-quality brochures and spoke remarkably well on his subject.

At this point, the insurance guy was standing about a foot taller with his chest at full expansion and a grin from ear to ear. Then there was deathly quiet as the lead was asked which one he had bought from and why. He replied, "Oh, I went ahead with the other guy because he seemed to have exactly what I need." The smile disappeared from his face but he was very gracious in defeat. The point being that these days it is extremely common for salespeople to try to quickly determine what it is that they think people want, and then by pressing the emotion button try to shoehorn the people into their products and services.

Intensified needs are a far stronger buying motive than a dream is. Selling really big dreams can lead to issues later down the track. Analyse all the scams on the Internet from Nigeria. You will find that all are designed to hit the 'big-dream' button of some poor unsuspecting person who has not managed to make their own dreams work. The frauds dwell on people's emotions, and peoples missed dreams. This is abhorrent.

I heard of a person who has, as yet, not been so fortunate in life. In his early 50's, he suffers from a crippling disease with no known cure. He has recently been the victim of a scam, and no matter what anyone has said to him or warned him about this he has bought into the supposed promise of a big-dream outcome. So much so, that he has now convinced himself that he is soon miraculously going to get a free five million dollars deposited into his bank account, and a budding African wife to go with it. He sent them about four thousand dollars of his friend's money, his driver's licence details and his bank account. You may think I am pulling your leg with this story. Sadly, I am not. Hard to believe isn't it?

At last reports, he is still waiting, for the money and the bride to arrive. I just cannot believe that he has been so badly scammed. Meanwhile, somewhere in Nigeria many people are sitting around laughing their heads off having taken some poor person's life savings. Shame on them. Make sure your solution to their needs is achievable.

Not one for selling the lofty dream, or leaning heavily on people's emotions, I am a salesperson, who looks for how I can help someone else win in both their business and personal lives. If they hire me to help with their sales, then my goal is to help them improve the bottom-line, fix their problems, and make sure that they get the recognition and acclaim. Eventually, they will most likely introduce me to their friends and associates. We all know that people usually hang out with similar like-minded people who will respect each other's decision-making. That makes the sale so much easier to achieve. In my experience, it still applies that buyers consistently choose to do things that they think will provide the most benefit at the least cost. Here, is how we go through proven stages to get to, 'Yes' by defying them to say, 'No,' and to get paid.

Need is what you have spent the question time in the 'discovery schedule' uncovering, and you have already advised them that if you can't help them, then you will be the first to say so. During this question time, you will usually uncover many needs that the prospect never actually realised they had.

When you are writing down the answers that the prospect has provided to your questions, the key is to look for their specific words and expressions. It is a big mistake to believe that you know their vocabulary. Even in a highly technical business, you must still use their words. Who is it who believes their words - them. So when you come back with your final proposal dotted with their exact own words they are unlikely to discredit them. Need works both ways.

Let them know that you want their business. Let them know that you will fight hard to get the business. Ensure that you will keep whatever you hear to yourself, but that the questions you are asking are designed to make sure that you offer the truly best business solution that you possibly can. No prospect will ever throw you out when they know you are working hard for both their business and your own. After all, they want to know that you going to stay in business for any after sales service matters that may be required.

No Desire.

Desire definition: to wish or long for; to want, or to express a wish for. A request, wish, or longing. There is no chance of making a sale if there is no desire on the part of the prospect. Plain and simple! You must disturb them so that they realise, regardless of your proposed solution, what they are going to miss out on if they fail to act. You need the prospect to realise what the consequences are if they do nothing.

In an effort, to create a desire by disturbing, be careful to not just manipulate their desire by making the prospect deliberately dissatisfied with what they have and with their lives. Think, for instance, of the way that creating the desire to own them has led to the relentless exposure of violent video games to children that in my mind has helped incite the increase in playground bullying. When creating desire with your prospect you should ensure that it is done ethically and results in the creation of responsible desire.

In other words, make sure you are not in any way harming your prospect and only ever leave them in a better position for having met you. It's all a matter of respect. You don't want to encounter your past clients, or anyone else you've sold to, on a golf course and they chase you around brandishing a three wood because of some damage you have done them!

It is essential to have positive consequences then you can also sell tomorrow and the day after that. Positive consequences for an individual might mean doing some good for their lives, families, and consciences. For business people and professionals, it might mean doing some good for their bottom line as well as your own. Sustained profitability, social and environmental responsibility are now expected. Companies are becoming more aware of ethical issues. They are taking some responsibility for the influence that they wield over them. There are even purpose-made ethical and green investment funds with benchmarks so that money will not be invested in companies that cause harm to people, animals, or the environment.

I have conducted specialised sales and management training assignments with companies who have since come under the scrutiny of the ethical spotlight; in particular manufacturers of tobacco products and poker machines. You could also add to that chemical, pharmaceutical, oil, mining and brewing companies. It's a fine line that keeps slowly shifting. Only you, your conscience, and corporate governance can be the judge of the ethical values of the service or product that you sell. In my case standing in low ceiling training rooms for days on end with, twenty or thirty sales executives from a tobacco company all smoking was some justice.

Fixing roofs and wall cladding every day for some years, cutting, drilling, handling, and hammering sheets of asbestos, wearing only jeans and a tee shirt could yet prove to be terribly expensive punishment, as well. Safety equipment was barely heard of, and certainly not mandatory back then as it is today. In retrospect, maybe I have paid my dues.

No Hurry and Importance.

In the 'discovery schedule,' appointment hurry does not mean hurry up and buy. Hurry means for each specific need that you have uncovered knowing the date they need to be solved by. Then how important is it to solve each specific need. The needs that are both urgent and important are the greatest matters that you then focus on. Whether your prospect is a business or a private individual the issue is the same, it is the difference between what is actually happening right now and what they desperately want to be happening right now. If the difference is only negligible, then there will be no hurry. If the difference doesn't help them to a better business result or better private life, then there is no importance. Therefore, no solution, no matter how meritorious, is needed.

To establish hurry you must determine how valuable finding the solution is. To do this use questions that require a specific answer that relate to urgency and importance such as "What's the most important priority to you with this? Why? What other issues are important to you?"

To establish, importance, you must determine what the consequences to the bottom line or their personal circumstances will be if they do not proceed.

No Money.

The objective for the salesperson is to offer a solution to the prospect's most pressing most important and most urgent needs. In nearly all occupations, these needs are measured in dollars. The crunch of the sale will always come down to dollars. What is the dollar value to the client for solving the specific need? Money is up there with oxygen in any business decision.

154

Salespeople who sell at the lowest price will always be the pushiest, and they will always want to get in first. In the sales cog system, my objective is to give the best possible solution that I can. Consequently, I am usually the highest price option hence I put so much more time and detail into my sales effort. We all know as salespeople that, behind-the-scenes, someone in administration is keeping track of us. The feedback given by my clients to administration follow-up is nearly always words to the effect that I've been particularly thorough, but may have been a little too long winded.

Often, managers try to change that in me, but I say to them, "Did they buy? " In addition, touch wood and cross fingers, my strike rate for closing and settling is always up there with the best of them in the team. When 'The price is too high', comment comes up; I ask them sincerely which part of my service would they like me to leave out to get the price down.

Every successful salesperson understands the motivations of the buyers of their product or service. Economists, psychologists, and marketing experts have studied and analysed this topic to the point of exhaustion. Here, are two rules of thumb. Selling any product or service to another business for resale or to be used in the running of that business, the prime motivation is money.

Your prospect will buy your offer if it increases profits or reduces expenses. Business likes and needs a profit that's its main reason for being. Be smart, and build your presentation around the fact that the reason any business that buys anything can be explained with the desire to make more money, and see how successful you will become.

On the other hand, when selling to the public, you will discover that motivation to own a particular product or service is tied to emotions. And there are many, pride of ownership, comfort, status, fear, enhancing popularity, sense of accomplishment or sense of belonging-emotions that will put money in your pocket if you craft a powerful appeal to interest and desire. If you doubt this, study the advertisements of successful businesses - see how they structure their message around emotional themes. When is the last time you saw the ad for a new car discussing compression ratios or torque? No, it is romance, speed, and pride of ownership, all emotional appeals.

If, you learn to integrate your understanding of buyer motivation with questions, you will uncover the interests of your prospect. This may inspire them to buy your product. Do this, and you discover that your selling skills will rise to the top of scale, as you master the use of questions to establish trust and build interest leading you in to the confidence of your prospect.

Make sure that the only promises you make can be kept. Delegating can be an effective way to save time but can also put sales at risk. As a salesperson, you are ultimately responsible for what you have said to the customer. Once you have delegated a task, then follow-up to make sure the task has actually been done to exactly, or exceeding the promises that you have made. Once you have lost them customers are exceedingly hard to get back. Any accountant or business owner will tell you that getting a customer in the first place is costly. Getting the customer's repeat business is where maximum profit is realised.

What habits must Pat improve, to go from mediocre to champion?

When I was with Pat, he spoke so fast that I found it difficult to both understand and keep up with so I think the speed and volume at which you speak also has a lot to do with trust.

Speaking in staccato is a no-no and yet it was what I witnessed many in-house trainers doing. They are speaking unusually quickly in order to try and get through their material in time. Slowing your words down just a little will speed your sales results up and I am not talking about killing the enthusiasm in your voice. I'm simply saying slow down a little bit. The best way to test this is to record your own voice while in an actual sales environment to check it.

Pat promised to follow-up, with the documentation to keep them happy and pacified at the time. He then delegated that task to an administrative person. When this happened, the client picked him as a person whose word was not their bond. The delegation was expedient to Pat but very expensive because he lost the customers trust with that one single action. Pat should consider new ways to:

- ❖ Speak at a coherent, comprehendible speed.

- ❖ Match the prospects tone.

- ❖ Leave nothing to chance, by following everything up.

- ❖ Have stories that bring the client into the moment, the here and now.

- ❖ Then have stories that take their minds ahead to future possibilities.

Chapter 27. **Team Approach:** Strength, security and safety of numbers.

One thing I have learnt about building client confidence and trust is that it is better to have a team approach. Even the self-employed or independent commission earner for a large company doing everything can still demonstrate a team approach. They can do this by asking others around them to help. Clients tend to worry when there is only person there. They may have serious concerns over matters such as who they deal with or what they do if something unfortunate happens, the one person becomes ill or takes time off from the business. All these thoughts hover in the back of their minds.

When on your own in a business think of ways to build your team numbers up. Maybe have a couple of freelance friends who can be affiliates, or perhaps a spouse or family member. Create a small group that will both inspire, and add the appearance of being more than a single sole operator.

Selling, at times, can also, be a lonely existence, and when you're alone your mind can easily drift towards self-destructive negativity. All on your lonesome is hard, so get into networks with like-minded people. There are plenty on the Internet; Virtual Assistants can be hired for only a few dollars an hour from selected overseas countries. Hire a personal, business coach. They are everywhere on the Internet. Similarly, you could hire a business mentor. You can also use the organisation that I'm part of, as sales mentors via webinars if you choose.

These people can be essential components of your team; then the client feels assured that no matter what happens, they will be OK. Those in business on their own should be applauded for being entrepreneurial. People love buying from self-employed people. They love to deal with the person in charge. They know that they don't have to struggle through multiple levels of management and numerous evasion tactics by head office subordinates. Their preference is to deal with the responsible decision-maker, and not the subordinates who can hide behind company compliance matters. With online technology, today, small operators' can outperform the many, much bigger corporations because they are often bogged down, with lots of different agendas. They cannot act and change as fast. The bigger the ship the longer it takes to turn it around.

What habits must Pat improve, to go from mediocre to champion?

Pat represents a large organisation that manages many billions of clients' money and wealth. By the nature of their business, in order to maximise returns for all concerned, it is essential that they have many highly regarded analysts and financial experts. Every client's intimate financial details need to be shared by others. Pat should have explained this to the client. No matter how big the organisation is, it should not be assumed that clients would trust them. The client should always be assured of the safety of their confidential information and their documents. Things like photocopies of passports and drivers license details are prime targets for computer hackers and thieves these days. Pat should consider new ways to:

❖ Use his team for problem solving and finding solutions.

❖ Develop a sense of security about client matters.

❖ Disclose the events of the meeting accurately to his backup team, warts, and all.

❖ Build his company's good reputation and integrity strongly in his prospects mind

Chapter 28. **Gently, Does It:** Withdraw and set the closing

Now, let's go back to the initial 'discovery schedule' meeting. By this stage, 55 of the 60 minutes of your allocated 'discovery schedule' appointment has now passed. The appointment is ending. It is time to tie down on the next meeting and gently withdraw, leaving the prospect almost aghast that you haven't as yet tried to demonstrate anything to them like every other salesperson who manages to get through their door have. Just as you are going out the door look back over your shoulder at the prospects face and they will be sitting with their mouths open in surprise.

To tie down the next appointment, first the salesperson should summarise the events to date. Actually, I am yet to meet a potential customer who doesn't like talking about themselves and their lives and their businesses. When I point out the time that has elapsed, on nearly every occasion people say to me, 'that's fine Phil just keep going until we are finished.' Think about the last time you went to dinner with friends at their place. Maybe those friends had been away on a special holiday.

During the evening, they took out their recent holiday snaps to show you. You sat there most of the night smiling, occasionally mumbling at the right moments. You had to look interested the whole night, whilst desperately trying not to nod off to sleep. When you eventually left at the end of the night, and they saw you off at the door with a big wave saying, "come again soon," guess what those people said to each other about you after you have gone.

My bet is they said, "Gee what a lovely person. We must have him, or her, back again." Now what did you say to yourself in the car? My bet is you said something like, "Gee how boring. I must try and avoid repeating that experience." The same applies when a salesperson goes to a potential client and talk's non-stop about themselves and their product. The client has the same reaction as you did over dinner with the talkative couple. The power of the sale is in the ability to listen, accurately identify and summarise the client's needs and fulfil that need by making the client a considerable amount more profit than you make yourself.

In the COG system that I use, we recommend you adopt a team approach. Following the initial needs analysis, you then ask the customers permission to take the needs that have been identified back to our team, so that you can prepare a team solution and bring it back to the customer in a presentation proposal. You should also seek permission to complete your 'discovery schedule' with a physical survey of the client's premises. Then, ask permission to uplift any of their product brochures and the like, that may assist your solution.

Explain that your proposal will include actions to be taken in the field, or on their premises. Actions such as; sales audits, and client visits with their sales team members. We ask if we can pre-set that date for the next meeting, and it is always within 4-5 days of the interview. Otherwise, the customer has forgotten what they have told you, or a second salesperson had got in before you and sold them a different solution. Worse, they have gone elsewhere and bought others' product or service.

We are also very careful to describe our solution as a proposal that is specifically tailored to their unique requirements and not just as a quotation; the expression quotation suggests that several others will also be quoting.

We also like to join in client visits with their best performing rep, their middle rep and their worst rep. Going with each to, personally visit their best clients, their middle clients, and the client who they last lost, or one who they don't like to visit. Those visits forms part of our solution, they allow us to be very specific in tailoring it with exact case studies and results to work with. We also visit the branch offices; many there offer a different perspective than those operating at the head office.

Going out on these visits is a fun time. The day always starts with the client company's representative in a polite but apprehensive mood as we visit their best client. This client often coincides as their favourite client. All is fine and dandy and we hear the client tell us how great the rep and the service are over tea and biscuits. Then as we are driving away from that successful meeting, we can see the rep feels warm and fuzzy inside. Like the cat that just ate the cream.

Then, we ask why they have just driven past a business that could be sold to, or who the last client was that they lost was. We then ask them to take us back to the business we just passed. You can imagine how things rapidly change. All jovialness is instantly out the window. The steering wheel is gripped a lot harder, jaws clench, and sweat appears on the brow. You would be amazed how many times we can salvage that, once lost client, for the rep or obtain new business.

This ends the initial discovery schedule meeting. Thank them for their valuable time and insight. Reinforce the importance and the urgency. Clarify how best to communicate and set the date for the presentation meeting and establish that all decision-makers who need to be present will be. Ask for those people's cards for your database records so that everything relating to their name and personal details are accurate.

Segment Five:
Preparing for the
Closing Meeting

Chapter 29. **Research and Demonstration:** Go beyond the norm.

This is where the hard work starts. Be careful when doing your research. Please, do not just do a Google search, everyone else is doing that. Use libraries, newspapers, University, Technical Colleges, and industry gurus, and controversial people sites too. Remember the accepted norm is not always going to remain true. Earl Nightingale told me that in the 1880's, when streets were lit by whale oil before the light bulb was invented, the newspaper headlines read, 'World to go dark, now that whale blubber extinct.' People believed that, thank goodness some radical thinking came along and invented the light bulb. Add some of those people's controversial ideas into the mix as well because you never know they might be right, and it demonstrates unbiased analysis from you.

Bread was first made thousands of years ago, but it wasn't until about 250 years ago that a controversial nobleman named John Montagu was gambling and didn't want to stop to eat. He asked his servants to put some meat between two slices of bread and the sandwich was born. This nobleman's title was the fourth Earl of Sandwich. Industry Gurus, although they can seem frightfully authoritative, are never right 100% of the time either.

Irving Fisher, highly respected Economics professor, Yale University, in 1929 stated; "Stocks have reached what looks like a permanently high plateau." Likewise, with positive articles, balance them with negative ones. This shows that you that you know about them and are not frightened of the negative ones.

When writing your proposal, you should take special care to ensure that every issue you raise passes the, 'so what' test. In other words, if the salesperson says something that the client can respond with the words, "So what", and then the salesperson has failed the test. I was out on observations with a salesperson that I had been recruited to train not long ago. When this particular salesperson asked one particular question that obviously did not pass the test I almost burst out laughing. Quick as a flash, he jumped in and answered the question himself. Saying to the prospect, "That's a so-what question, sorry let me put that question another way."

We laughed about it over coffee after the meeting. Many salespeople just do not understand this test. They go right into long recitals about features and jargon, but to me a client should clearly identify with the solution as matching or bettering their current situation.

The prospects all know what their problems are, that is always the easy part. What they don't know is the solution to those problems, which is why they are waiting with baited breath for your presentation and proposal solution. The solutions are what they will invest in. The better your solution is, the bigger the investment they will be prepared to make. Use your team as a mastermind to help you prepare. Two minds miraculously create a third when working in harmony and unison.

Let every team member contribute equally without disruption. Suspend judgment by resisting the urge to let everyone know that you've tried that before and it didn't work – so what hero? An improved version of it might work now. Get all ideas out first then sort them into what you want to keep and what you want to dump. How badly does Australia's retail scene need this approach of re-thinking and refreshing?

Chapter 30. **The Retail Experience:** Times are a changing.

Hey, Australia is too great a place to rant about too many things not going well, but I feel that some of our retail shops are way behind the world on customer-focused sales skills. Go into most big retail outlets and you get the feeling that you are simply interrupting. The standard Australian retail welcome; "You right there?" sounds flippant and condescending. I get the distinct impression that staff are under instruction to give priority to restocking shelves and completing paper work.

You feel as though they have been instructed to wait for someone more important to serve than you. It can be a most unpleasant experience. That is a problem with many management structures, where the top dogs are more interested in profit margins and can easily become out of touch with the consumer.

The consumers always take the first available opportunity to bite back. No wonder Australian consumers have gone to the Internet in droves. That must be a real worry for retailers. Some of the more outspoken ones, who have boasted when times are great and now whine when times are tough, are even suspiciously accusing the Australian consumer of just using them as a fitting place to try out the merchandise before buying on the Internet. They are the management who always seem to look for faults in their own staff performance.

"Hello?"

That is a live customer in front of you, who has taken the time to do research and then battled traffic and parking spots to get to your shop. They want human interaction. I hear that as a cry from the customer for help, an opportunity to lift your game. Might just be time to stop grumbling, throw the 'one size fits all' compliance manuals out, teach your staff some good professional selling skills, and turn the shoppers into buyers.

Think about arriving at some of the bigger stores. I generally go there on a weekend and once parked the first people I encounter are the kind-hearted folks from various charities fund-raising outside by barbequing sausages. The sausages are only a few dollars. The problem that I have is that I rarely carry any loose change; it rattles in my pocket and falls out. Instead, I have a debit card tucked neatly and securely in my top pocket.

I get a bit embarrassed explaining this to the nice charity raisers and wish them luck. Then, after a few more paces I encounter 'security', who is usually someone big with an official looking imitation police uniform on. Their presence screams to me, 'Watch out buddy, we think you are going to nick something, so we are here to deter you.'

They obviously do not trust people entering their shops, and no, like most of the population I don't shoplift. The law is enough deterrent for me. This off-putting entrance experience is tantamount to having a large 'welcome' mat out with the words, 'Oh no! Not you again - watch yourself!' Then I ask for directions to what I want to buy, and get told an aisle number.

When I get to that aisle I rummage around, pick stuff up to measure it or study it, then have to hunt around to find the place I picked it up from and so on. Seldom does anyone offer me assistance unless I ask for it. Once I finally find what I need I go to pay, and there is a conga line of people with stock under their arms all queuing at the one counter that remains open. I look around to see if I can spot where all the other checkout operators have gone, perhaps it's the long break. This experience is repeated in many of the larger shops that I go into.

Buying dynamics are changing. New challenges are out there. As a typical consumer, I want an interesting and fulfilling experience that stimulates me and makes me feel good about the store and the purchase. The in-store experience has to be better than the online experience. There is great scope for implementing a fresh approach; nothing too radical needs to be done. Management should concentrate more on looking for, and finding, something that staff is doing right. Praise them for that.

The security should be just visible enough to deter the few ill intentioned, and not the great majority of honest, decent shoppers. How about the store paying for the sausages, by way of donation, to the hard working voluntary community workers cause? This good-will gesture of a 'free' sausage could be returned many times over. The Charitable donation might even be a legitimate deduction. In exchange for that hot-dog, while I eat it I would be happy to fill out a small questionnaire, or enter a competition that requires me to explore the whole store. Give me a pen and card to fill out my email address, preferred method of communication, and reason for buying. Why not have suggestion boxes there as well?

I know that sausages are standard fare so how about a nice spit roast instead to be different. The local butcher can promote his shop on the side of that. Then a nice piece of bread complete with pork, some crackling, and apple sauce would be the outcome. Same effort required for a way better result. At the door replace the big 'security' person with a smiling, greeter; the 'Director of First Impressions.' That person could even dance the Highland fling, I don't care just cheer me up. That person could have a clipboard with some questions for me that only take a few seconds to answer, and show the shop cares more about serving me than it does about grabbing my money.

The store should then push the experience as their point of difference in their marketing and advertising, as opposed to always just the price and product. Get a check out express lane going and have something there to take my mind off the long wait. Instead of having $2.00 grab items near the checkout have something to capture me as a long-term Internet client as well. Maybe I could join their stores 'Internet shoppers club' while I stand there, or sample a biscuit from the local bakery with a special offer. That way, you are promoting your non-competing local traders and generating more good-will.

Chapter 31. **<u>Be Confident:</u>** Acknowledge your Competition.

Please, resist the temptation to make any derogatory remarks about your competition or opposition. Speaking ill of your competitors, in a deliberate attempt to make them look bad can have the opposite effect. It can result in a negative reaction towards you. Especially if part of what you say, causes a red flag to go up in the prospects mind.

When someone says something to me that is negative about another person who is not present, I think twice. I immediately wonder what they are saying about me to that person, or others, when I'm not there. It is far better; to briefly acknowledge the presence of your opposition in the market place. Say something mildly positive about them, whilst keeping a straight face, and then move on to the advantage of dealing with you.

Be familiar with your opposition's business. Take the time to know what competitors are doing, improving, offering, and saying. Know their product, and know how they move. Keep well informed about the difference between their business model and your own. Remember, they are out there knocking on the same doors. Give your best shot at beating them to the sale, legitimately, honestly and with integrity.

Occasionally, when I am trying to catch a really big fish, like a multi-national company, I might practise on one of their smaller local competitors first. This way, I can really push the smaller competitor with some hellish in-depth probing questions and get all of their objections out so that I can prepare for the bigger event.

Of course, the fun option starts if you then get both clients at once and the bigger client wants exclusivity. Conflict of interest may disqualify you from dealing with one of them. Pick the client you want to run with, and bow out gracefully from the other. Leave the door open for another day.

Segment Six: Preparing for the Closing Meeting

Chapter 32. **A Bucket Of Gems:** Your winning Proposal.

I suggest that when preparing your proposal; choose a plain font like Arial. Fonts are always a flavour of the day proposition, but I find Arial size 10 or 11 is both readable and presentable. You should then submit the hard copy of the proposal in a good quality spiral bound folder with your own stationery or white paper, not just in a pocket with paper clips. This is cost effective, and you should display your company logo and livery on the front cover.

Provide each of the key decision-makers, with their own personalised originals. Provide a soft-copy version also for those decision makers to refer the proposal to their micro managers with ease if need be. Also, have an unbound loose-leaf version. Then hand out one page at a time to consider, and tie down as you progress.

Take your time when writing your proposal; remember they have probably seen dozens of other proposals before. With this in mind, be imaginative, hard-hitting, and slightly provocative. Demonstrate how your solution tackles their real issues. Speak to the prospect using their words exactly as they spoke them at your first 'discovery schedule' meeting. Select the right words: expand your vocabulary.

Look for the right words to use when trying to convince a prospect to buy from you. Their pre-perception may be that all salespeople are too ambitious, or used to pushing, so your words can either win or lose prospects in a heartbeat. Fill your presentation and proposal with punchy, memorable, explicit key words and phrases that benefit and provide a solution to your prospect's needs. Not ones that just give away your desire to make a sale. Prospects must easily understand your words, so avoid becoming too academic in your approach. One academic said to the other, "I say dear boy have you read Marx?" To which the other responded, "Yes, I fear they're from the cane furniture."

In your presentation, avoid any words that you may be using that risks making you look amateurish. Take out all the "umms' ", "ahhhs'" and "oh yeahs". Remove any colloquialisms, and eliminate obscene language and change language that could be interpreted as racist or sexist. Remove any words that might be considered discriminatory or offensive. Try to avoid making the out-dated gaffs that the Duke of Edinburgh is famous for.

Insert some concise key conclusions. Great comedians do this with punch lines, some of which I have remembered years later. That exceptionally funny Scotsman, Billy Connelly, knows the art. When he was asked which words he wanted on his tombstone, Billy responded that he wanted inscribed in; eight-point type, the words "You're standing on my balls". I heard him say that about twenty-seven years ago. Often, that is the length of time that your prospect, will positively remember you.

Your headings and subheadings should be concise, accurate, of similar scope, and brief. The order of pages should be:

- **Front Page:** On the front page of the presentation pack place a colour photo or a graphical representation of your proposed solution. Convey a connection by having your logo beside theirs and check your logo is never bigger. Seek their permission before using it. Represent their logo, entirely in accordance with their corporate or business branding. I once made the mistake of cutting off part of a very famous logo to make it fit my presentation and wow was I given a mouth full.

- **Letter of Introduction:** In the front, there should be a loose leaf, unbound introductory letter thanking them for the time and attention given to you at the original appointment. The information that they willingly shared with you about their current situation and the opportunity afforded for you, to subsequently present, your solution to their business is also acknowledged. Add, 'the following document provides a detailed look at the solution to…' (Whatever, you have discovered as being their major needs)." I like to assure the client of two more valuable intangible matters; my best efforts at all times and my promise of confidentiality.

- **Contents page:** As with the entire document, you should have this page set up so that the short cuts are enabled in the soft-copy version. Any micro-managers who are given the document can then navigate their way through to find their specific area of interest with ease. Then no one can later make the claim that it had been held up on, his or her desk, or lost. Help them get to the exact topic they want in the document as quickly as possible. Some micro-managers believe that their whole purpose in life is to prevent executive decisions being made, especially if it involves a change that they suspect could rattle their own cage. I think it is a myth that people resist change. People only resist change when they fear the consequences. They love change that they can see is for the betterment of their lives. Therefore, 'change' like most other concepts needs to be sold to people, in a way that they look forward to it happening.

- **Executive summary:** All key decision makers will read this summary and base their decision on it to proceed, or otherwise. They may only scan the rest of the document, jump straight to the investment page, or never read it all. Provide key decision-makers with an email PDF copy for distribution. The summary page should contain your name and contact details so that it can be viewed as a stand-alone document. Being the most salient part of the summary, ideally it is best left till last to complete as it summarises your entire proposal in as close to one page as possible.

- **Discovery Schedule:** This is a report-styled document detailing all the key points that you have identified, from the prospect's needs 'discovery schedule', during your initial discussions and asking of questions. Use as many of the exact words that they used as possible. Avoid industry terminology here unless you have it correct.

- **Physical Survey:** This summarises how you conduct your survey, handle the matters that you might uncover during your physical survey and observations of the various company people and clients who you are visiting during the inspection. This survey then assisted in tailoring your final deliverables to their needs. Often a sales audit is included.

- **The '(Insert Your Company Name)' Solution:** This description of your solution links directly to the main points in the 'summary of discovery' that the customer has raised as issues. From your 'intensifying' and 'tying down the need' segment, you have identified the priorities. List your solutions to each issue in bullet points here in the order of importance and urgency exactly as the client has detailed to you. Obviously the matters that you have established as being both very important, and very urgent, go to the top of this list. State the following; "Listed below are the priorities you have indicated, and we have addressed them accordingly."

- **Features and Benefits:** In this, the largest section, provide a detailed description of exactly how the solution meets the client's needs. Every element, or step, involved in the solution must be included here. Please make sure that every issue from the discovery schedule is covered. Take the three most prominent ones and make sure that your proposal goes into some depth as to how those vital needs are handled. Wherever you describe a feature, you must also describe what the benefit of that feature is. Use words such as 'which means', to describe the benefit of that feature in as clear and precise way as possible.

This allows you to express the impact of your benefit as a dollar amount on the bottom line so that the cost of the investment can be easily justified. Make sure you can deliver on everything in your solution that you claim. It is imperative that the decision maker, who has given you their time and confidence, gets a winning feeling from introducing your solution. Any subsequent negative consequences from any part of your performance or product and service could be disastrous for both them and you.

- **Timetable for Implementation:** The timetable expresses in formal language the critical path for the installation of your solution. It must make a strong statement demonstrating that you are well organised and aware of the different functions of their business model. Demonstrate in chart, or mapped, form for their convenience. Express key points in practical terms, detail achievable and believable outcomes. It should specify a start time, and finish date and record all those people involved in both their team and yours. Stress that the timetable is approximate only and that it may take longer than you think. Show the consequences of any extra costs and time if needed.

- **Other Issues:** Subsequent to your discovery meeting include other matters that you thought of that were not raised and feel will add benefit to the client's solution. Special features or ongoing commitments may be an example and should be described in a two or three sentence summary of the issues and the solution to them. Photos help to support this.

- **The Investment:** Cost is a highly significant factor that influences the buying decision. Give an itemised breakdown of your professional fees, charges, labour, service, or goods etc. Express the 'deposit' amount as an initial investment. Show taxes and levies as an additional amount. Spell out the anticipated ROI (Return on Investment) from your tangible and intangible benefit statements, to ensure your prospective client puts value on them.

- **Payment Plan:** Detail any finance options that you have available and express them as a total, then break these down into the lowest possible amount. Such as $ X per week. Provide a checklist for them to tick their preferred finance options.

- **Terms and conditions:** These should be presented in the same size font as your proposal otherwise the client will have a thorough search under a microscope for the small print demons that so often seem to appear after the fact.

- **Agreement:** This is the signing document. As it is legally binding, it should be entitled accordingly. Your legal counsel will inform you. Examples include, 'Heads of Agreement', 'Consent to Proceed', 'Contract to Construct.' It must also include all required signatures, details, dates and titles. Bind each contract into a quite separate document if it is longer than a few pages, otherwise your presentation document will be too bulky.

- **Your Team:** Provide brief capability statements about any members of your team who will be directly involved in the solution. Their names, titles, direct lines, mobile numbers, and email addresses should be included. Include other staff for backup if necessary.

- **Additional Matters:** At the back, add other features and benefits of your product or service that might not have been identified or discussed. This gives the customer added confidence that the salesperson certainly knows the buyer's business. This section could be entitled "extra features that will enhance your business model' or 'business operation' or whatever is most appropriate.

Please set up and use templates for efficiency, but as a professional salesperson, be careful about just going select all, copy, and paste. Take the time to read every proposal from cover to cover, spell check it, and recheck their names and phone numbers and then actually dial the number to double check who answers.

One, ultra-embarrassing, incident happened to me because I had taken a short cut and not double-checked a proposal that still sends shivers down my spine whenever I think about it. We conducted tailor-made sales and management training assignments for a major brewery with hundreds of hotels and retail outlets. The work was conducted at regular intervals spanning over twelve years in total. We had many templates set up for their work. When I arrived to present a proposal to a very different organisation in a quite different field, I had been uncharacteristically unprofessional, blasé, careless, lazy, and not bothered to double-check my work.

Half way through my presentation, of the proposal, one of the decision makers suddenly asked me what the brewing company had to do with this proposal. There to my horror was the brewer's logo and company name embedded in the proposal. The only reply I could think of was to congratulate them on noticing it and then light-heartedly said, "Well it was put there deliberately to see if you were paying attention. Well spotted." That got a wry smile. We moved forward once I had then explained the error and apologised. Fortunately, they proceeded, but I ate humble pie over that blooper on several occasions. Lesson learned.

In summarising the proposal content, it should contain the clients own words exactly as they were spoken and have all the needs that they identified. Do not miss out any needs because although you have identified the priorities, it does not mean that a key person of influence along the line necessarily agrees with those priorities. The one that you miss out could be the most important in the mind of the key influential person. Avoid using the expression 'among other things', because it sounds as though you may have left something out that could potentially have a sting in the tail. The most impact that you can make on a client is to talk just about their business! Here, is the contents page from an actual investment property format that clients of mine use:

❖ Location information:

❖ Why that particular location.

183

- ❖ The closest city.

- ❖ Specific suburban.

- ❖ Location maps.

- ❖ Past sales in the area.

- ❖ Sales statistics.

- ❖ Demographics.

- ❖ Site plan.

- ❖ Floor plans.

- ❖ Scheduled finishes.

- ❖ Rental appraisals.

- ❖ Depreciation schedule.

- ❖ Photographs of the site and the buildings.

- ❖ Recent property articles.

- ❖ All contact details.

Chapter 33. **The PowerPoint:** Let technology add the crunch.

This segment of the sales cog is almost every modern salesperson's strength, but there are a few sometimes neglected, but none the less important, elements that you should remember to include in your presentation.

Technology should never be used as a crutch, to fall back on. Any technology that you are relying on should only ever be a tool to support your solution. The presentation should never direct the sales interview. It should only ever support it. I have personally never seen a client jump up after a PowerPoint presentation and buy, who has not first been helped across the "bridge" and into "buyer" mode. Once, and only once, they are in this frame of mind can you consider proceeding to any demonstration of the features and benefits of your product or service.

The problem with this approach is that the presentation rarely addresses the specific issues or concerns of the buyer. Because their needs have to be addressed, there is no compelling reason for them to consider. If you want people to buy from you, give them a solid reason. It needs a personal connection to gently, and genuinely, persuade them to become a happy and satisfied buyer. So many salespeople just sit behind a projector and talk to the screen. It is always better, if possible, to have an interactive demonstration. Use the actual product, and highlight the features and benefits that are specific to the client's unique requirements. These were identified in your discovery schedule prepared by you at the first meeting.

Telephone system sales companies are enjoyable to watch doing demonstrations. With their superior technological capability, they can have high consumer involvement demonstrations of all the latest technology complete with the client company's actual logo and name on the screen. They can also add a voice mail setup with their details already featuring. Customer involvement is the key so not just talking at them but having them thinking it is already theirs is paramount.

With PowerPoint, you can run a little show in the background with company logos side by side while seating arrangements are being sorted, hands are shaken, and tea and coffee arrangements made. Tailor the presentation, specifically to the prospect and their specific requirements; it is a colossal mistake to always use a generic presentation.

For me, it's most powerful when we put an older more experienced head that has been knocked about in the field for years together with a budding more technical savvy Generation 'Y', or 'X', who knows how to perform magic with presentations. There is an optimum mix, between old-school wisdom and new generation ideas, which produces far greater things when combined. Find this potent mix and use it to your advantage. The junior technical whiz may well have a better feel for market trends such as Facebook and Twitter and the use of apps.

I was getting a haircut the week before last, and my barber received three cancellations whilst I was there. He immediately used an app to notify anyone within 5 km of his shop saying, he had three cancellations, and he was offering a 20% discount to the first three people that came in the next hour or so. I was sitting there and in they came holding up their phones and asking for the discount, so it's a completely new world and long may it last.

On each slide, have their logo and your logo together. This then implies a subliminal union between the two companies. Where you want to include, pre-recorded material, such as; video clips from YouTube, or website links have them inserted inside the presentation on a separate split screen. Better still utilise an additional second screen. Nothing looks worse than flicking in and out of the master PowerPoint presentation, especially if the link or Internet connection fails when you need it.

188

The salesperson should take into consideration the amount of time each PowerPoint presentation takes to prepare. Please, don't simply copy and paste, and then just change the logo for each new prospective client, think again? It has taken you considerable time to organize and conduct the original "discovery schedule' meeting. Having gathered information that is immensely powerful for your presentation, use it judiciously. This should be presented in the order of importance that the client has identified for you, and then expressed in priority of importance, urgency, and lastly dollar benefit.

Whatever solution you are offering, the client must eventually determine a major benefit to their bottom line and return on investment. In the case, of private individuals they must see huge dollar value at some time in the future that far outweighs the investment to them.

I saw one case recently that horrified me; a Business Development Manager had been given some four months notice of an upcoming conference where he was to present to future major customers. Yet only two days out from the meeting, he had still not prepared anything and asked a junior associate to prepare him a detailed PowerPoint Presentation. The junior associate prepared it as requested. The BDM then delivered the presentation, but from his lack of proper preparation, the Business Development Manager had no idea what was on it.

During the presentation one member of the potential clients team, a mining company, asked about cargo handling facilities at the Port of Dampier. To which the Business Development Manager answered, 'I'm not thoroughly versed on this, I'll have to come back to you.' Two slides later, it turned out that the junior had actually added some real detailed slides about cargo handling facilities at the Port of Dampier. Right there, for all to see, the salesperson revealed that he had not thoroughly rehearsed the presentation beforehand, let alone know what any of it was about. The Six P's of Selling still applies, 'Pre-Planning Prevents Piss Poor Performance'.

Directors and Business Development Managers can sometimes hide behind PowerPoint Presentations, and run the risk of portraying a weak image to the customer. Salespeople and Business Development Manager's who genuinely understand what they are talking about just use the PowerPoint Presentations to illustrate additional details. They use visual aspects only to support their arguments, and to brighten up their performance.

Chapter 34. **Aim For Perfection:** Practise your presentation.

Ask any golfer. Practice makes perfect and perfect practice, leads to perfect performance. Instead of sitting around the coffee shop, grab another salesperson and practise your presentations with each other. A sole operator can video themselves or ask a spouse or partner to video them. Whatever the circumstances, just do it.

Then, from the video replay carefully examine your own movements and see what needs to be improved on. For example, are you waving your arms around too much or worse still are you pointing your finger at the prospect. Never point because it is an extremely aggressive action to take. The old sales trainers used to say, "When you point at someone, you have got one finger pointing forward at them and three pointing back at yourself". The same applies for hand movements.

Check to see that you are not gesticulating, showing the backs of your hands, or thumping the table. Do as the preachers do, when asking for donations, hold your hands open. This hand signal has always been associated with good things like trust, honesty, and allegiance. Never do as police do when instructing you to stop by showing their palms held up and facing you with fingers pointing up. This hand action has always been associated with negative things like stop and don't go further.

Chapter 35. **Study Seating:** Recognise hierarchy in seconds.

The seating arrangements are also worthy of note. In the 1950's, a man by the name of Julius Fast studied and wrote about the art of body language. Since then, many have borrowed and enhanced his material. He wrote an in-depth account about the skill of seating people in various positions depending how you want to deal with them. Movie producers know this.

When there is a cops and robbers movie, watch how the defendant is seated in the police station when the good guy bad guy cops are at work and trying to extract a confession. Usually the bad guy cop is leaning aggressively across one side of the table while the good guy cop sits to the right of the defendant and offers him a drink. Occasionally the bad guy cop storms around behind to intimidate him.

Think about the seating arrangements, when in your own family situation, you sit down around the table for a Sunday meal, Christmas dinner or a special event. At the risk of stereotyping, this example applies to the average family. The main dining table is usually rectangular. The father, who sees himself as head of the household, sits at the head of the table. (In much larger organisations, this differs and is usually the middle.) The mother most often has done the bulk of the indoor cooking.

She will place herself, with her back towards the kitchen, in the seat nearest to the kitchen. This seat is at the other end opposite her partner so that she can easily stand up and go to and from the kitchen. The eldest child is usually seated to the right of the father. In the case, where there are grandparents they may be to the right of the father as well. Often, the youngest is seated further away from the father to the right of the mother.

Whenever you are presenting in a boardroom setting the same unspoken rules apply. There are many books on this subject for reference. Often the CEO will sit at the top end of the table. The person who does much of the day-to-day work, such as the General Manager will sit at the other end of the table. Just like at the dinner table, seated to the right-hand side of the CEO will be their right-hand person. That is where the phrase came from. Seated on the right-hand side of the General Manager at the opposite end will be the person of least importance.

Use this person to your advantage, as a sounding board. Generally, they are the one person in the room, apart from you, who is trying the hardest to impress the CEO and the others. The CEO may think of that person as the least important in the room. So, if you need to get an objection out at any stage, look to that person in the weakest seat.

Ask them the right question to bring that objection out, and the fact that it is that person asking will have the effect of devaluing the importance of that objection before you deal with it. By doing this, the biggest objection has been put on the table by the least regarded person. Get that person to offer their opinion on that objection.

Often, the others in the room are somewhat reluctant to agree with that person, so the probability of the rest of the room agreeing with you increases dramatically. That is your objective. You should sit in the middle with your back to the door. The reason for this is that, the wall with the entry in it is usually glass, and if it is not photo-chromatic, or the curtains are closed, you may be distracted by people walking past. For the same reason, you would try not to be seated with your back to the window because you want people to pay attention to you and not be distracted by what is going on outside.

I learned this lesson the hard way when presenting to an audience in a mirrored glass building. From the inside, looking out they are a window and from the outside during the day, they are a mirror. There I was conducting my presentation for a client with my back to the window and wondered why everyone suddenly burst out laughing.

Thinking that what I'd said was not really meant to be funny, I turned around and beheld a well developed woman on the street outside. She was using the floor to ceiling window as a mirror to tidy her hair, and adjust her undergarments. Blissfully unaware, she was entertaining a room full of people. It occurred to me, at the time that I could have raised my fee had I had prior knowledge of her entertainment factor.

What habits must Pat improve, to go from mediocre to champion?

In Pat's position, it was a little more difficult, as the dining table was against the wall and he only had three sides to take into consideration. The male sat at the head of the table with his partner sitting directly on his right-hand side. Then Pat sat himself down and asked me to sit at the end of the table opposite the male.

Had he sat in the middle of the two of them, he could have been far more effective. Then, when they encountered the problems before their own eyes on the laptop screen as the presentation progressed, he could have made a reassuring statement like "Now, how can we overcome this challenge together." In reality, the way he had them seated had pitched them against each other.

With the couple sitting that way, all you will end up with is an argument between them. Whereas seated in between them he would, figuratively speaking, have been able to hold his arms around them as though all three of them were united as a team. In that, 'us versus this enormous problem' scenario, highlighted on the screen in front of them, Pat would have gained additional rapport and considerable trust. They would have then been comfortable to ask him to seek a way for them to overcome and resolve the issue.

Also, the cats crawled all over us much to the amusement of the prospects. These constant distractions took away Pat's control of the situation. It would have been better if he had tactfully asked them to be put both the cats in the other room for the duration of the meeting.

Pat must consider new ways to:

- ❖ Quickly analyse the power seating position

- ❖ Have disruptions limited to as few as possible

- ❖ Make the presentation work for him, not him for it.

- ❖ Get away from sounding like he has a rehearsed script

Chapter 36. **Closing Meeting Preparation:** Going for Gold

This is the event where the rubber meets the road. Timing is essential as you risk losing control of the sale unless you come back within five to seven days of your initial discovery schedule appointment. Any longer, and people will have forgotten what you are all about. At one stage, I had quite a bit to do with a Mr. Hal Krause from the mile-high city of Colorado. Hal was an initial pioneer of American Sales Masters. He is a lovely person and he is the absolute master of making energy work. I queued with Hal once at the Denver Airport in Colorado.

On this occasion, we were travelling together and lined up about 10th or 11th in the queue for the counter, Hal had enthusiastically handed his business card with a special discount offer for his sales training products to everyone in the queue before we reached the counter. He just felt it did not matter how many cards he gave out, as some of them would respond. What a champion. American Salesmasters, who were early movers in the sales training industry in the 1970's used to have three criteria set for this meeting; they were something close to this:

1. That there are no interruptions, all phone calls are held and assistants are asked to not interrupt.

2. That all the decision-makers required to say 'Yes' are there.

3. When, and if, those decision-makers decide to proceed, they will agree to a payment of no less than 20% initial investments by way of deposit, there and then.

Tough approach isn't it? However, it worked remarkably well for them, so let us now take a closer look at the logic behind this approach.

1. No interruptions.

We know that many people in business are hard to get hold let alone meet with so, make the most of their time. Some businesses even have signs on the front door that require any visiting salesperson to have a preset meeting time. We also know that the potential client we are endeavouring to sell to may have set up an opportunity to escape during the sales meeting by pre-schooling their PA to call or knock with an interruption.

To insist on no interruptions is difficult to obtain and takes skill. You will get knocked back in which case you make light of it, but once you have learnt how to do this it is a very useful tool. You find out at the outset how serious the potential client is on listening to you as a sales representative. Use words to the effect that, as a courtesy to that potential client, you will turn your phone off and politely ask them to do the same and to hold any incoming calls until you have finished.

Time management is crucial here too. As I said earlier, I hate the approach of asking for fifteen minutes of their time unless they have questions. Unless you are selling a low-cost, simple, item then this is nowhere near long enough, and I think that the potential client will mark you down in their mind for taking this approach. To me it is much better to ask for forty-five minutes, and then stay to that time frame. Should they wish to go over that length of time and talk further then great! They will ask you. When they do, obviously they are very keen on hearing what you have to say.

A good friend of mine, who has done very well for himself in the sales profession, likens the sales process to taking someone out to dinner who you would like to get to know a little better romantically. First, you pluck up the courage to ask that person a question such as, "Can I get you a drink"? Then relax them with some general questions and small talk.

Following this, you might ask them out for a dinner date. He says, (with tongue firmly in cheek), that if you get a lunch date then that's tantamount to a job interview, and if you get breakfast then you're either out of, or in luck depending on where and when the breakfast is.

So, when you are asking general questions over dinner you may then start being more specific with questions such as "Would you like to meet again?" Now at this point if the other person says yes, like Meat Loaf's subject in the song, you manage to progress as far as third base. However, if you are then suddenly interrupted, the next time you meet you cannot just jump right back in at the third base, you have to go through the warming up process again. Lots of salespeople forget this. When you start the next meeting you must warm your audience up again.

When phoning to confirm the proposal, presentation and demonstration appointment it pays to ask if they have spoken to any of your competitors about these issues as well and whether they have finished looking at the competition products or services. This means that they are then free to make a decision on the day. The idea here is to eliminate the issue of a deferred decision because they still have other competitor's options to look at.

In my experience, people who sell on price like to get in first hoping that the customer will not then waste time by seeing the competitor's product whereas my consultative system means you can command a higher price provided your service and quality are better.

2. Decision Makers.

Lots of hours are wasted every single day by salespeople who offer their products and services to the wrong person. Especially when salespeople rush out to visit anyone who calls without first doing at least some pre-qualifying. The thing that makes me grimace the most when observing salespeople is when a prospect that has been presented to comes out and says, "look I am really the wrong person to deal with" or "I will have to take this further up the line.

Just leave your proposal with me and I will show it to the people who matter." Imagine if you will, your presentation being made to the person further up the line by that person. They will simply never deliver your presentation as well as you can, and unless they are excited about what you are offering, they certainly will not have their heart in your presentation.

The chances of you making a successful sale from this 'hit and hope' approach are zero. Then, you are forced to make the decision, having spent all this time, how much further you keep working on this potential client. This can cause all sorts of problems especially if your sales management has pencilled that client in as a likely sale.

In most countries, hierarchical management still exists. Whenever possible, it is better working from the top down. Once again, it is a matter of courtesy. If you ask for all the decision-makers to be present they most likely will be, and they will feel as though you are treating them very professionally. It is also a sign of confidence when you are comfortable presenting to a group of their key decision-makers and that you think it is important to submit your solution to all of them. So prior to the meeting, ask your contact person in the organisation to email and confirm that all decision-makers will be available. The same applies in smaller business make sure the partner is there if they are, in any way, a part of the decision.

Way back in time, after I first finished on the tools and was invited to be part of management I was sent out on my first sales call to deal with an old very well established joinery company about 20 kilometres from our office. I remember being very nervous and straightening my necktie several times. I had never worn a tie to work before it was most uncomfortable.

When I arrived at the joinery, business there was an older man out the front busily cleaning the windows. I can see him now in my mind as clearly, as though it were yesterday. I interrupted him a bit hastily and asked him quite bluntly if he could direct me to the boss. He pointed to an even older man cutting timber on a bench saw a way down the back of the workshop.

I proceeded down the factory, past the workers, and presented myself very politely to that person. Excusing myself for being a few minutes late I treated him with the greatest of respect. He looked at me strangely and said, "No mate I'm not the boss he's the bald headed old bloke out the front cleaning the windows".

I sheepishly made my way back up to that guy cleaning the windows, who I now knew to be the boss. Wow, he berated me with a very stern lecture on how I should treat everybody in his workshop as though they are the most important person in the place. I apologised as best I could and tried to explain it away as my first sales call. He advised me to always treat everyone in the business as though they were the most important person there, a valuable lesson. I took his advice and this early, on the job, lesson has stuck with me ever since then. No doubt, he has long since departed this earth, but I am sure he would be pleased to know that his philosophy is still being well heeded.

To further reinforce and add to this point, many times I've witnessed salespeople befriend the business owner or person in charge of that division and ignore or handle that person's assistant differently. Things change in business quickly and often the person's assistant becomes the boss. When that happens, unless they have been treated well by the salesperson, guess what, that salesperson is out the door in the blink of an eye with instructions not to return.

Take the cleaner, and the managing director of the same company away for a fortnight and find out who would be missed the most. Remember, everyone is important no matter what their job is so treat them all with respect. When one of my sons started as a mail boy for a big corporation, he met one of the top executives in the lift one day. The very well dressed executive noticing him with the mail trolley said respectfully, "Ah the mail boy, I had better be nice to you because they can often become the boss." Nice touch, my son was delighted.

3. Understand Closing.

Unless you close, you are not paid. Nor is the company who employs you paid. However, to get to the point where you can successfully close, you must have first done everything correctly. Sorry but, there are no magic closes that can make up for poor prospecting, poor qualifying, poor discovery, poor demonstration, poor product knowledge, and poor handling of objections.

Closing is the sharp end of the sales process. It is the part where even the slightest hiccup means that you will be feeding the ducks instead of sipping champagne that evening. Salespeople who cannot close are merely commercial visitors, and there is no line on any corporate balance sheet with any upside financial benefit for corporate visitors.

Take for example, Vessel Charters. Large sums of money involving millions of dollars per transaction can be involved. There are very short time windows in which to act, as the vessel owners usually only allow 2-3 days for charterers to make decisions.

There are also often lots of terms and conditions that are not standard for each charter, so they often need either changing or negotiating at the time of shipment. The Business Development Manager or salesperson needs to be very assertive, confident, and persistent when getting information and funds from the customer as time and space is of the essence.

The client always needs to be assured that the selling company has the ability to manage the risks involved and complete the shipment effectively. The Business Development Manager needs to follow up relentlessly and close the deal before the ship-owners 'close the gate' by selling the space on their vessel to another shipper or the ship sails. Business Development Managers, who fail to secure charters, are those who hesitate to call the customer about difficult decisions that need to be made. Those who lack the attention to detail to pick out flaws in the ship-owners offer and fix them quickly.

Those with the inability to satisfy the customer that both they and their business know what they are talking about. Those who are not brave enough to explain the real risks, and dangers of shipping goods by sea on a chartered ship. For example; delays, weather, strikes, and mechanical failure can all contribute to delay and loss. Being unable to answer such questions as a Business Development Manager, or continuously communicating back and forth with an expert to answer customer's questions contributes to lost sales.

Here is a recent, example of how a salesperson, BDM failed to secure a charter.

Customer: Goods to ship in Containers.

Cargo: Accommodation units.

Ship Owner: Large International Commercial.

The Business Development Manager did not obtain the full requirements of the cargo movement from the customer (he simply did not ask the right questions). Nor did that manager hand the shipment over to the operational department experts but rather attempted to arrange everything by himself, despite not totally knowing what he was doing.

The Business Development Manager let considerable time pass between the customer requesting the shipment and contacting the shipping company. He also failed to check the details of the shipping company's proposal and portray these effectively to the customer. The client wasn't followed up diligently enough to get additional details about the cargo that ship-owner asked for.

The client was given too much leeway with payment terms; a deposit would have clinched the arrangement. Late replies to email, and condoning everyone in their business having a look at the agreement and adding their opinion delayed the close. The ship-owner, threatened to arrange another cargo if the agreement was not signed. The Business Development Manager thought that was just a ploy, and delayed further.

The ship-owner did fix another cargo and the deal was lost. The customer had to book on another ship that had to reposition to carry the cargo. They paid another 30% on top of the original price. Neither party had a victory.

There are many books about 'closes', you should read a few of them. Roger Dawson wrote a great book entitled, 'The 29 Secrets of Closing the Sale'. Those of you, who are serious about cranking your income up, should crawl over broken glass to get a copy of this book. It includes such classic closes as, the 'Puppy Dog Close,' 'The Power of Suggestion Close,' and the 'Fulfilling Your Dreams Close': all essential closes of the professional salesperson. I spent a few days with Roger and his lovely wife Geisel at his California home in the mid 1990's; He is an Englishman who has made his fortune in the USA. We share the love of steak and kidney pies.

Segment Seven: Show me the Money - The Closing Appointment

Chapter 37. **Final Meeting:** Getting the team ready to proceed.

After having left, the 'Discovery Schedule' meeting with permission to proceed to the presentation here is what you must do immediately in order to deliver your presentation and proposal on time. You need to hit top gear and start scoping this sales presentation while it is all still fresh in your mind. Remember your total solution is in filling that difference between where the client actually is at that point and where they ideally want to be. The three main objectives that you now have to satisfy the client's needs are:

1. Your solution must meet your client's requirements.

2. You must establish a budget (cost of sales).

3. You must deliver the solution on time.

That is now your goal.

Start by gathering your team in; make sure they all know who the project manager is and get agreement on a visual overview of the project. Immediately decide on each member's role. If you own your business, that's cool, it just means that you have to fulfil all these roles.

What I do, when working on a project alone, is have some different coloured hats and put the name of that role on them. For example when I am writing I have my 'Tonight Show' hat on and I imagine that Jay Leno is interviewing me. My answers need to be good or he may make fun of me in front of millions.

Then, when I do the proposal I put on a 'Banker's' hat. This puts me in the frame of mind where I am deliberate, considered, and very serious. You wear a different hat for each different role you need to cover. By now, you are probably rolling about the floor laughing with tears in your eyes, as I am thinking about you doing that, but hey- it works for me.

These roles should include such things as; shared responsibility, task oriented, time and schedule constraints. Look for team-oriented players who bring different 'tools' and skill sets, who you know you can trust and who give you mutual support. Keep the open-minded and flexible natured themes going throughout the project. Obviously, you need to keep in mind your own company structures, governances and authorities.

Give the team the problem, factually and clearly stated and give them the solution that you know that the client is ideally seeking. Tell them where you think your opportunity to help lies and any constraints that may exist. Once you have established this foundation, then you can agree on priorities and usually, logical and rational conclusions. Make sure everyone understands these objectives and define the final deliverables, or outcome, so that everyone knows what has to be done.

Factors to determine the success of your proposal include:

❖ Calculate a measurement method for the success criteria.

❖ Know when your contract is completed, with a start and finish date.

❖ List all your assumptions, risks, and obstacles.

❖ List the tasks required to complete.

❖ Break all tasks down into logical bite-sized chunks.

❖ Determine the resources that you need to complete.

❖ Estimate the duration of each activity.

❖ Allow plenty of extra time for unseen and unexpected events or items.

❖ Plan and schedule the work.

❖ Add any additional client requirements that might crop up.

❖ Double check for unrealistic estimations.

- ❖ Detail the people that you will involve in their solution and why.

- ❖ State the benefit to the client that each person's different skill sets bring.

- ❖ Describe how each set of skills closely fits the client's needs.

- ❖ Show any facilities that may be needed.

- ❖ Detail how availability might impact on schedule.

- ❖ Choose which of your success stories from satisfied clients matches.

- ❖ Money, include all expenditure. This is a key element.

We also provide a map of the client solution. It shows everything broken down graphically expressed as a pie chart, flow chart, and a graph. The mapping includes all tasks, activities, and time-frames.

You know the ones with squares and arrows that represent the relationship between each task; there are templates available on Microsoft's site. If you would like to see a fully customised sample of a flow chart that you can refer to when necessary, you are welcome to get a free copy at www.salesdrive.com.au.

We also like to attach a list of every resource and a person's name who will be contributing to that specific solution.

Your solution must be the best one and must stand above the rest. Make the conclusion a serious 'call to action.'

What habits must Pat improve, to go from mediocre to champion?

A confident person in front of a client gives off an air of unquestionable competence. Pat, on the other hand was slouched in the chair and gave the company's canned presentation. It felt like he did not want to be there and was just going through the motions. He looked at the wall and the screen, not at the prospects.

He skipped over a few slides because they did not apply to that prospect. He seemed bored and wanted to rush through it. The prospect wondered what they had missed seeing. His call for action was all about paperwork gathering and lacked any plan that gave the desire and the motivation to stir the prospect into action. Pat should consider new ways to:

- ❖ Involve his team in the skills needed for presentations

- ❖ Communicate client needs more precisely to his team

- ❖ Understand that everyone involved in the solution is equally important

Chapter 38. **Delivering Your Presentation**: "You're on!"

Your professionalism is never as much on display as it is at this meeting. Follow sound business etiquette, dress well and arrive in reasonable time. If you have travelled internationally for the meeting then check for differences in custom and modify your actions accordingly. I neglected to do this research and once made a presentation in Osaka, Japan where proceedings commenced with a lunch for all the key executives. Here, I was sitting there wondering why no one had started eating, then the director sitting next to me pointed out that they were all waiting for me, their guest, to start first. Oops!

Switch your mobile phone off. Try to keep the meeting about half way between formal and informal. Ask your prospective client if there is an established seating arrangement and stick with it. When seeking feedback, or fielding questions allow the more senior people to contribute first. Never interrupt anyone, even if you strongly disagree. Show you are well mannered, courteous and considerate. They are all busy people, and you are fortunate to be there so make sure you start and finish on time.

Before starting the presentation most salespeople run around checking the lighting, drawing the blinds or curtains and laying out paperwork. The audience has seen all of this before and often been bored many times as a result. Overcome this by getting there early and setting up. Use the conveniences before you start the presentation. You want your business to stand out, don't be like everyone else. You want to win a sale not a marketing award so keep bells and whistles to a minimum. The usual PowerPoint presentation is over-used in a business environment, but it is different in a private demonstration to non-commercial people.

Think differently, and be different. I went to a presentation on goal setting when I first started working after leaving school; it was a very new concept at the time. Too many years ago to mention the date but to give you an idea it was held in an old World War II hangar that had been converted in a warehouse. The audience sat there staring at a blank wall when suddenly an arrow whizzed over our heads and bounced off the ceiling then onto the front wall before landing in the corner on the ground.

Thinking the next war had started we all ducked for cover. Turning around, we could see striding up the aisle a well-groomed older man holding a cross bow over his head and shouting, "That's what happens when you don't have a target. You might never hit anything." Then he painted a large target on the front wall, walked back, and fired another arrow and it hit dead centre, 'bulls-eye', making a slight thud as the suction rubber tip stuck to the wall. Then he strode back proclaiming how important having a target is.

It was arguably the most relevant, unexpected, maverick, powerful opening to a presentation that I have ever witnessed. There was nothing high tech, obscure, contradictory, too clever, or offensive, just right to the point, (pun intended). It got everyone talking to each other all giggling nervously. Get your team together and mastermind the presentation, think outside the square.

A word of warning here, should you go late into the night masterminding with a few light libations to help lubricate the flow of creativity, please make sure it passes the 'next morning test'. That test means that when you review all your great ideas from boozy sessions review them the next morning sober and if they are still as good, then use them. Judging by some of the messages posted on Twitter some might wish that there had been a built in 'next morning' test.

Depending on budget and the potential profit to be derived, you can be creative without being expensive. We were chasing a $1,800,000 contract and we sat around in one such creativity session. Our plan was to have two of our younger staff members, a male and female, dress up in very fun attire as though for a Hugh Hefner party at the Playboy mansion.

We rented the costumes and had their hair and makeup professionally done. They were then delivered to the client's uptown office in a limousine carrying three items between them. We had arranged for the prospects personal assistant to greet them and have our prospective client's executives in the reception area just prior to knocking off time the evening before our presentation meeting was due to take place.

On arrival, they smiled and handed the three key executives the beautifully wrapped parcels from us. The first was an individually boxed champagne flute each. The second was a bottle of quality champagne, on ice in a silver service style ice bucket. They popped the cork with the usual flourish and theatrics associated with important occasions. They were invited to toast our pleasure at looking forward to the next day's presentation, just as they might prior to a big sporting event that was occurring next day that they would all be attending. As they sipped their drink, each was curious as to the last parcel and finally could not resist enquiring as to its contents.

The third parcel was a wooden box with a glass front that had the words, "In case of emergency break!" Inside was a leather-bound version of the Holy Bible. Taken aback, and with their curiosity heightened our couple assured them that without our solution then prayer might be their next best option. They took it in the light-hearted spirit that it was intended and we presented to a very attentive audience next day. Fortunately, we were awarded the work, and subsequently kept that client's business for many years.

Apply the 'so what' test to your proposal and your presentation, no matter how interesting you might think it is. Do not bombard your audience with too much technical jargon and information, only have punchy relevant points. The detail has been covered in your accompanying proposal.

A dynamic, never to be forgotten, business presentation has to captivate your audience. They don't care about the presenter nearly as much as they care about themselves and their company. But, if the presenter is poor they will think the same of your company. Like I have recommended with your sales appointments practise your delivery over and over. Take out all the imperfections.

Most of all "KISS", keep it simple salesperson. Be natural, work the audience one at a time, in a natural manner. Leave humour out, they haven't come to laugh; this is a business presentation. Use a simple prop that conveys a powerful message and exemplifies a key point or theme like my arrow man did. Talk about them and your solution expressed as Return on Investment. (ROI).

Most of all never leave people wondering what you said. Explain terms and acronyms if you must use them at all. It all comes down to what your audience walks away with in the end. Did you deliver another boring business presentation? Or, did you persuade or motivate everyone to action?

Chapter 39. **<u>The Sharp End:</u>** Potent proposal presentation points.

From your presentation, you are now ready to go through your spiral bound proposal. Handle them with matchless pride as though they are gold. When you believe they are gold so will the prospective client. For 'gold', read as meaning something scarce and of immense value. Just like your solution for their needs.

Don't just shove your proposal document under their nose, or leave it on the table in front of them. Handle them in a way that the client desperately wants to get their hands on it. Hand the loose-leaf letter out first and give them a moment to read that.

You explain to them that the purpose of that letter is to recap the discovery schedule meeting and remind them of the needs that were uncovered.

Warm them towards you again slowly as you remind them of the priorities and urgency. Ask if anything has changed that you should know about since your last meeting. If it has, then turn right back to uncovering and intensifying the need again. Keep your bound proposals on the desk with you, and then recap highlights from the 'discovery schedule.'

Then open one bound proposal, and extend it out just far enough to have the key decision maker reach out to get it. Hold it firmly while you highlight the contents page and ask if that looks as though you have covered everything. Wait for a positive response, when they reach for it, let the decision-maker take it.

Appear slightly reluctant to let it go. Be subtle; do not over react, or you will be out on your ear for stupid behaviour. Once they have it their hands then they 'own' it. Be methodical, tie-down on every page as you go. No one should have to refer back to an earlier page. Once you have arrived at the Investment page it is time to close.

Chapter 40. **The End Game:** Closing the deal.

You must know how to ask for the order and have confidence in yourself, your company and your product and service to be sure that what the client is paying you for will reap them a financial reward far greater than the amount you are asking for.

I prefer to soften the word 'sign', which rather conjures up thoughts of 'signing your life away' in the prospects mind by using the word 'authorise'. Here are some examples of closing techniques used by salespeople that you should modify to suit your individual circumstances. Take these suggested statements, adapt them to suit you, then commit them to memory and practise out loud until you can recite each one of them verbatim in your sleep.

Direct Close: Where you just ask for the order.

- "Can I have your authority to proceed?"

- "When would you like delivery?"

- "Can we sort the paperwork out?"

Assumptive Close: When you use your company Order form to close.

- "Can I confirm your address details?"

- "Would you please authorise this application?"

Either Or Close: Will you go ahead or, when will you go ahead?

- "Would you prefer the smaller one or the larger one?"

- "Would you like the blue or the green version?"

Half Nelson Close: A term used in wrestling when they force their opponent into submission by twisting the others arm half way up their back. This is generally used after the prospect requests something. Keep the arm-twisting limited to your imagination.

- "Will you go ahead if we can provide that?"

- This will either expose a real objection or lead to a direct close.

Benjamin Franklin Close: Also known as the Duke of Wellington Close: Where you re-cap on all of the benefits. Take a blank piece of paper and a pen and set it out like my diagram below.

- "Let's put out the facts for you ..." Then help them to complete the right-hand column with prompts from your benefits:

- "How about our...."

- Say nothing and leave them to complete the left-hand side: "So, what reasons can you think of that would prevent you proceeding today?

- Leave them to complete on their own without your help.

Cautionary Tale Close: What happens if you don't proceed?

- "Can you afford to jeopardise your vital communications for a few dollars a week?"

- "With the cost of labour these days, can you afford not to have time control?"

The Lost Sale Close: Ask the prospect why you failed, ask them for help to improve your selling skills.

- "Would you mind telling me where I went wrong?"

- "Would you mind helping me?"

- Instead of saying, "No" to your previous close attempts, the prospect will now say; "No because ..." 'No' to me just means that they want to 'know' more. It is called selective hearing. I can easily hear, 'Yes' from 200 metres, but am deaf to the word, 'No' at 2 centimetres.

- Now you really know why you lost the business and there may even be a chance of salvaging the situation once the objections are sorted out. The dialogue is still alive.

Process of Elimination Close: The close for the prospect who won't give reasons for 'No'.

- "I feel there is something that you're not satisfied with.   Is it ...?"

- Start with things you know the prospect is happy with; get those 'Yes's' rolling.

- This close may lead to the Duke of Wellington Close, or the Lost Sale Close.

"I'll think it Over" Close:" Thank-you that pleases me because you wouldn't be thinking it over unless you were really interested. So that you have all the facts while you're considering ..."

- This close may lead to the Duke of Wellington Close, or the Process of Elimination Close.

The Final Objection Close: The aim is to obtain the prospect's agreement that there is only ONE reason for not buying and that you have correctly identified it. Listen to the objection right through to the end; make sure you fully understand it.

- "Is that all that is causing you concern, or is there more you would like to know?"

- "Is that of particular importance to you?"

- If you can overcome the objection, go to the Half Nelson Close.

- If you can't overcome the objection, go to the Duke of Wellington Close.

Most Important! As soon as you have asked a closing question say nothing, keep as quiet as a mouse! Let them answer; the power of silence is golden and puts pressure on them to respond. Do not speak, do not scratch, do not adjust yourself, do not cough, just keep quiet, still, and remain calm. If you do not speak first, then your prospect has to agree to either go ahead, or explain why not.

Many times I have witnessed salespeople say something like "Oh, by the way, there is one other thing that I have thought of that I meant to tell you?" Please never say that, because all you do is buy it back.

Any salesperson who does this at the point after the client has given the 'go ahead' and signed, immediately buys it back! To look at it graphically, diagram 'D' shows how the GOG takes an opposite approach to average sales methods. Once you get familiar with COG, the close becomes almost automatic. Simply ask if; "they understand everything and are happy to become involved, or is there something else that they need to know?" That will mean you are given the go-ahead or you are about to hear their final and most serious objection.

Diagram 'D'

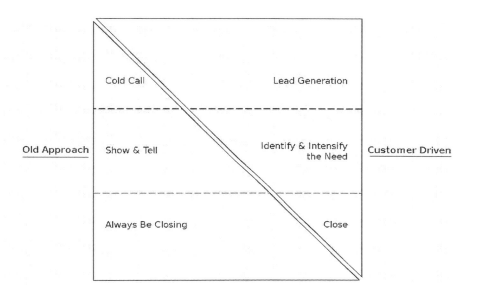

Once you have been given the go-ahead you must secure the arrangements by seeking a payment for the initial investment. Arrange to have the payment made by direct deposit into your account and have the bank transfer receipt printed for you or emailed to you.

Conclude by thanking the client for their business, assure them that they are in safe hands; yours, and confirm all communication methods one more time.

Some salespeople have difficulty discussing their price. They feel they have to justify or defend it and become very uncomfortable. They prefer to drop the price, rather than explain the significant factors and then go on and win the business without cutting your own throat, pricewise. Don't try and avoid discussing the number that is on the page or skip over it onto something else.

Segment Eight:
A Sale Isn't a Sale
Until The Payment
Clears

Chapter 41: **Following Up:** 'Buyer's remorse'.

When a sale of significant value has been made, all salespeople have to be aware of is the next event in the process which is known as 'buyer's remorse'. Buyer's remorse is an emotional condition where a person feels remorse or regret after a purchase. Logic goes out the window.

It is frequently associated with the purchase of higher-value items which could be considered unnecessary. It may also stem from a sense of not wishing to be 'wrong' or, being made to look foolish. This remorse occurs to a greater degree with private individuals than with business people. It reinforces the need to have all decision makers present during the sale.

Online Business Directory has relabelled buyer's remorse to the more technically correct term "cognitive dissonance" and uses this higher brow definition: State of psychological tension arising from incompatibility among a person's attitudes, behaviour, beliefs, and/or knowledge, or when a choice has to be made between equally attractive or repulsive alternatives. One example is 'buyer's remorse,' a feeling of guilt associated with doubts about the advisability of a 'buying' decision that one experiences after making an expensive purchase.

Marketers try to manage these doubts with supportive information such as testimonials, money-back guarantees, and after-sales service. The consultative selling process, COG, has a unique method of dealing with buyer's remorse. The client is now no longer physically with you, and they may have spoken to someone else, like a close family member or your opposition who has talked them out of it or sell them an alternative. You will never know that unless you ask. Warn people who have just made a purchase from you that when they get home, or when you leave, they are going to experience buyer's remorse.

Explain that it is natural, and happens to everyone. Also, explain in some depth about peer group influence, or the well meant advice of others, then bring them back to why they are happy to have proceeded. Hand them a piece of your stationery and a pen to write down any reason that they come up with to panic or regret their purchase.

On that paper write your mobile number together with the words, 'Call me at any time I'm available for you 24/7." Then get them to fervently promise that they will call you 30 minutes after that happens. Why 30 minutes? Well, that gives them a chance to recognise that they are going through buyer's remorse. They will recap on all the reasons why they have bought, and hopefully they will ask each other whether it is necessary to call you. They will go back to sleep, or work, instead.

Reassure them that you would rather hear from them than not. If they don't call then, you call them in the morning and tie down again. Never rely on email to solve this for you; resolving buyer's remorse issues requires gentle human-to-human interaction. It has to be a personal phone call, maybe two or three but never email. Follow up sooner than you promised.

The sale needs to be re-enforced and strengthened. Email can never deal with the strong emotions that accompany, 'buyer's remorse'. Remember that a sale is not a sale until the payment clears so view this call as mandatory. When you miss one never let them know how upset you are, keep that to yourself.

As a fit, young buck, I did my time in the building and joinery Industry, truck driving, roofing, industrial wall cladding, and gyprock fixing. Then I went on to build my own houses and commercial construction through most of the next decade. I finally accepted the boss's offer of a management role. Those were the days prior to the invention of facsimile machines, mobile phones, computers, iPods, iPad's, and hand held devices of any kind other than a pencil or a pen.

The boss was a wily old Scotsman, and one of his first pieces of advice to me was, never post a letter that was written in anger. His advice was to write it, and then sit on it for 24 hours. After that time, read it again, and then tear it up. Any written communication had to wait in the queue at the typing pool. The typists then either queried or corrected everyone's work as they went, effectively acting as a filter. Now, everyone does their own typing, and the filter has been largely eliminated. Venting spleens via email is now all too common.

In many instances, salespeople take the easiest way out in following up a client. I prefer to put myself in the client's position, and consider how they best like to be treated. So, I ask them how they would like me to communicate with them. Like most people, I get numerous emails most days. Fine when it is from someone I know, or am expecting to hear from; I open and read them. The rest are deleted within a nanosecond. However, if the 'subject line' appeals to me as being something I need to know more about, then I might open that email.

There is a man in Sydney, Australia by the name of Dale Beaumont. Dale is going gangbusters advising on this subject. His program is called, 'The New Way of Doing Business' and I recommend his material to you. He is covering all things relating to today's best use of technology.

With small ticket or lower margin products and services, Internet marketing can work beautifully. However, with bigger-ticket items such as industrial capital equipment, property, investment, and financial planning I still believe human interaction face-to-face is the only way to maximise the sales potential. No doubt, ways to sell high-ticket items on the Internet will be perfected, in the future. Whilst the Internet is a lead-generating tool, you still ultimately need to put a skilled, professional salesperson face-to-face, toe-to-toe and eyeball-to-eyeball with the prospect to get the highest closing ratio.

The fact is that we will lose some sales, and there are many different reasons why this happens. When it does there's no sense in getting irrational, emotional over-reacting or blaming anybody else. It's still worth some attention. That lost sale may well become next year's best sale, depending on how you handle the follow up.

I like the sense of follow-up notes and thank you notes just to reassure them that I am still here. Ask them a few questions for some valuable feedback. I try and establish if they did run with a competitor and if so how were they better than us. At the stage when it is not salvageable, I just get on with the next sale by picking up the phone and starting the process again with a new prospect.

It is best to have a precise and well thought out plan for calling back clients. It takes time, but it does show the customer that you still want their business. It tells them that you haven't forgotten them, merely because they didn't buy off you at the time. When you are calling back, there is no sense in just asking if they got your correspondence.

Instead, ask probing questions about your correspondence, how they felt about it and can they see the sense in it. Salespeople that are more moderate simply ring back and ask if they are ready to buy yet. The top sales professionals, who I have observed, prefer to ask probing questions to find out where they are in the sales process. Maybe the signs are there that they have already struck a deal with your opposition, and that is why it has taken so much longer than usual. Have they returned your phone calls? How have they responded to you? Have you put too much pressure on them? Remember, they will never tell you if they just simply do not want to deal with you because they don't trust you.

What habits must Pat improve, to go from mediocre to champion?

Pat later followed the prospective client up with a standard company email and whilst a note is easy to do it needs to be handled with care. What I saw disturbed me so much that I asked the company to review all email sent on its behalf. The clients he had been visiting with had difficulty finding their paperwork. They could not provide a copy of their documents such as driver's license because they didn't have a scanner or a photocopier in their home.

For Pat to assume that they would open his email let alone read them, struck me as being way too presumptive. Pat also Cc'd the email to their work email. It is all very efficient use of modern technology, and you can do an awful lot of them in a short space of time. Had this been an email communication to a business2business client then possibly it would be sensible. However, to send a private email relating to confidential, personal matters to their business email address, especially if the person works in the public sector, risks offending either them or the email not being read.

In his office, Pat allowed me to read some examples of his follow-up emails. They were brief and to the point. Once again, great time management for Pat, but also risking that the prospective private client misinterprets that briefness as rudeness. Where the people had promised to send documentation to him, and failed to do so, his emails got progressively more frequent and terser. He had told his boss that one reason he hadn't got near to a sale that night was because they didn't have all the documentation ready.

Part of my role was to contact the prospect for feedback. When I re-visited them alone, and read the emails from the client's perspective, I felt quite embarrassed for him. My guess is that he was under the gun time-wise. As obvious as it may sound, these emails were costing the company lost sales. The next chapter details highlights of the matters that I pointed out; really this is a whole subject on its own. Pat should consider new ways to:

- ❖ Treat all email communication as part of the sale
- ❖ Start a new email instead of continually looping them
- ❖ Keep a watchful eye on work that he has delegated to others

Chapter 42. **Email 'Netiquette':** The modern dilemma.

On further review, I found that the person writing the emails to Pat's client was not a salesperson at all. He was a recent junior recruited into the IT department for his technical expertise. He had no skill or experience in sales. This certainly opened my eyes to the possible repercussions that might result from just one email. More alarmingly, companies send out hundreds of such equally unvetted, unprofessional communications every day.

All sent with one tap of a button. Is this a modern-day dilemma? I believe every document that goes to prospects, and clients should be part of the sales process. They should contain copy that has been written by a professional salesperson or copywriter. Review your email policy regularly.

The IT person had written to the prospect as though he was suddenly the answer to their prayers, without first going through the sales process. He had assumed the role of their paperwork 'police'. The prospect was surprised to be suddenly dealing with this new person on such financially confidential matters. They are hard-working people, and during week day hours, they cannot easily access private emails. They usually do so in the evenings or on weekends, but the IT guy had expected rapid response.

When this hadn't happened he kept firing out emails under his immediate manager's demands of him. At least 24-48 hours should have been allowed to elapse before following up. Once he had referred to an attachment, but he had forgotten to actually, attach anything. The more he sent the terser and to the point his emails became. The more he threw in industry jargon and acronyms the less intelligible his emails became.

Five emails later, he looked downright desperate to get the paperwork, and the more anti the prospect had become. The last one had several exclamation marks at the end, and as silly, as it sounds they took serious umbrage to this. The manager was also getting upset with the new guy. The junior was updating the situation with emails in a progressively less formal manner than he had done previously. He was talking to his boss via email as though the boss and he were best buddies. The email also looped Pat, his boss, and me.

When I approached the boss, as part of my sales audit, with my observations he was in the process of sacking another person who, whilst already on thin ice, had sent him a number of emails that were a cross between preaching and threatening. They were long and so voluminous as to challenge the Encyclopaedia Britannica. No doubt those emails were well intentioned. However, the manager translated them as being harsh criticism.

This particular manager had been a professional sportsman in a full body contact sport and the author of the email was a tall, skinny guy who looked so weak that he would struggle to escape from a wet paper bag. It occurred to me that he would never address the manager like this in a face-to–face conversation. Better to write more politely, as though the person was in front of him.

There were two instances in just two minutes of the extremes of emailing. From my association with that group I have noticed that my own personal email inbox has since been getting a lot more spam. What happens is all the names in the carbon copy (Cc) line are shown. Please, hide any looped emails in the blind copy line (Bcc). Summarise the contents in the subject line, and refrain from using words in all capitals as it is regarded as the online equivalent of shouting and besides that, it is more difficult to understand. Attempts at humour in the written form can be disastrous as the email recipient may well take it in a different light. Taking this argument to the extreme worst case scenario; as all emails are recorded they create a long paper trail, especially if they are looped in reply and then Cc'd to others.

Once that send button is hit, it is too late to recover. Indiscriminate or careless use of emails should be avoided at all cost.

Everyday newspapers reveal some form or other, of leaked email by political foes, aggrieved sports fans, or socialite informants.

For those living in England over the past 5 years, or more, you have hardly needed to bother answering your phone. Message bank could get it and the 'News of the World' would have emailed it to you later (brazen attempt at humour intended). Better to forget confidentiality in emails altogether and write them as though the whole world is eventually going to see them, because they just might!

Chapter 43. **Sales Form Recovery:** Fall down seven times, stand up eight.

Top performers in all endeavours have them the sales activity is no exception. Irrespective of the level they are at, all sales people at some stage experience a form slump. Sales slumps hurt both the fragile ego of the poor salesperson, and the bottom line of the company. These are unexpected events and often difficult to explain.

Never easy to comprehend, sales slumps can strike without notice. Management often assumes that the salesperson's overall performance is causing the decline. Sometimes they can be traced to a deeper personal issue, such as marriage concerns. However, it is usually only something small that is causing the problem.

Perhaps they have left out one particular part of their sales process. Many simply do not know how to correctly identify the missing elements in their own performance. They can often be seen throwing their arms up in despair declaring their entire performance is a mess. Just like trying to cook Granny's favourite fruit cake without all the right ingredients, say one tiny teaspoon of vanilla, only one small part has been left out. When this has happened morale slides down, self doubt creeps in, confidence wanes and mighty soon you can be in an overall sales decline.

Only careful, patient and thorough analysis will help determine the reason. It's a matter of management and sales working closely together. Everyone experiences occasional slumps the concern is that they don't recur too often.

What it boils down to eventually, is sales people who are in a slump have to just get up, shake themselves up and get over it. Then focus on more essential data about clients, and get on with selling.

"Anything you really want, you can attain, if you really go after it. Go for it now. The future is promised to no one" – Wayne Dyer

Plenty of times, I have seen evidence of how a decrease could potentially occur. On one occasion after a sales meeting, the people were all talking optimistically about how many sales that they will get in the coming month. They spent ages discussing all the marvellous things that they could do with the money they were going to make.

A cautionary tale that I can tell is about a member of a sales team who last year had by far his best year. What transpired was that it wasn't his sales expertise that had suddenly improved; it was his friendship with the sales manager who allocated the sales 'leads'. Unfortunately for him, that sales manager was suddenly demoted, and the new sales manager distributed the category 'A1' leads more evenly.

Meantime, that guy had committed himself to a brand-new top of the range vehicle, an overseas vacation, and a new house. Suddenly, his sales figures dropped dramatically, and he found himself way over-committed on all fronts. This reinforces the idea that a sale should only be counted as a sale, once the payment has cleared your bank account.

"Expenditure rises to meet income."
(C. Northcote Parkinson. 1909-1993. From 'The Law
and the Profits', 1960.)

Favouritism commonly occurs, when a company that started from scratch with a small, tight team experiences exponential expansion. The original team has formed a bond and stays tight in their group. Unless it is carefully managed, the new additions can feel somewhat left out. The problem is then exaggerated, because the new members start a clique of their own, then chaos reigns. Please, dissolve any factional associations as soon as possible, or the resultant sales slump will affect the whole organisation.

What habits must Pat improve, to go from mediocre to champion?

Pat's general conduct lacked the X-Factor. Very few top salespeople tell you how talented they are in the first few breaths as Pat did. Most of them prefer to walk the walk and let their results and others tell you how good they are. When I first met him in his car, I just had the first impression that he lacked a little bit of pride. It was obvious to me that he was not yet in the league of a top salesperson. Not that this is a bad thing. In selling if, you have someone with a few rough edges, it is easier to smooth those rough edges off than it is to take someone, who is too smooth and put on some of life's rough edges. In my case, maybe it takes a rough diamond to recognise a rough diamond. Pat should consider new ways to:

❖ Make an instant and positive impact on clients

❖ Let the runs on the board speak for his performance

❖ Learn to have empathy with clients

Chapter 44. **<u>Never Quit:</u>** Winners never quit, quitters never win.

There have been thousands of books published on the question of how to sell and related sales subjects; to begin with assess your own limitations. Perhaps ambition has gone, and you have already resigned yourself to the fact that a certain level is your lot in life. Maybe, you have lost the passion for your selling. Worse, perhaps you are feeling a little bit of anger, guilt, and resentment about the quality of your life.

Please, if this is the case, go down to the library and get out your pick from many self-improvement books. Start looking for the greatness within yourself. It is there, but to find it some just have to dig harder than others do. Start humming that song from one of my favourite singers; Bret Michaels:

'Every rose has its thorn'
Just like every night has its dawn
Just like every cowboy sings his sad, sad song
Every rose has its thorn'

In selling, the hardest of all psychological issues to overcome is probably the fear of rejection. It is hard not to take rejection personally. But, remember it is not necessarily you that they are rejecting, it is your offer. Get used to it; the only time you can be certain that you won't be rejected is when you are not out there asking someone to buy.

Some people will reject you, and you will never even know why. When it happens, I try to envisage them in the shower and that usually makes me chuckle for long enough to start thinking about the next sales challenge. Provided you have given it your best shot. Use as many ideas from books and others as you possibly can to add to your sales arsenal. Spend a few minutes thinking about a rejected sale and then let it go for another day. Your mindset should be, 'Good, I am now one step closer to my next sale'.

Like everything in life, selling has its ups and downs, so recognise that and get on with it. Many salespeople and sales managers, in my opinion, make the mistake of over analysing the sales opportunities that they have missed. I suggest you spend only a short time dwelling on the worst ones and many hours dwelling on the ones that you have had success with. This will cause you to improve your strengths and eliminate your weaknesses provided you have done your best.

Americans have a better attitude to failure than we have down under. When you are an entrepreneur or a commission only earner in America everyone expects you to fail a few times, but they will encourage you to get up and have another go. The Chinese are adept at that too. They have an old saying that goes something like, "fall down seven times, stand up eight". So if, you fail, rather than seeing that as a negative, take it as an opportunity to grow and learn.

Mistakes only become a problem if they are continually repeated. On the other hand, to put it another way; only a fool thinks that making the same mistake over and over will produce a different result. So just, avoid letting your own thoughts be the thing that sabotages your results. Zig Ziglar calls it 'stinkin' thinkin' and how right he is.

In sales teams that I have been involved with over the years, I have witnessed some absolute champions in action, some average ones and some outright duds. It has been my observations that the absolute champions, if they do miss a sale, never let that get them down. They just pick up the phone and get on to putting all of their attention and energy on to another one. More moderate salespeople, who have missed a deal often, go straight to the nearest bar and drown their sorrows. No doubt meeting a similar soul down there to drown their sorrows together; I've been there and done that. Misery loves company.

The top achievers know that even if their office happens to be a bank, there is no point hanging around the office looking for money. They know that there is no change lying around their office. The money is out there in someone else's office, but in order to make it, firstly you must have someone buy something from you. Not that it's all about money. He who dies with the most toys is nonetheless dead.

Being in Sales is challenging and there have been the odd occasions when I have thought about calling it quits or gone away on other endeavours. I sometimes think that I should have sought a more secure employment path. Whenever I feel like this, I try to arrange to meet with someone who is in a secure career. He is a close friend of mine and has been in the same job, with the same company, since he left school over thirty-six years ago. After about half an hour of talking with him, I realise that he is more tired and stressed than I ever am, and lost his spark some years ago.

This tends to do the trick and reignites the fire in my belly. Like anything, you honestly have to believe in what you do and love doing it to thrive. Knowing that, you help people to achieve their dreams and objectives, loving what you do and knowing that just around the next corner there is another potential client just waiting to meet you. That is what spurs you on.

"Never, never, never, never give up." – Sir Winston Churchill.

A merchant banker friend of mine rang me up one Friday morning when the global financial crisis first hit near the end of 2008. We used to have a "Thank God it's Friday" network lunch group that met on the last Friday of every month. He was quite dejected and wanted to go for lunch and have a few drinks to forget his worries. I could sense that all was not well as he told me he was being forced to sell his two-door soft top Mercedes.

Now when a merchant banker is selling his pride and joy you can guess that things are a little rough. I couldn't make lunch that day. Instead, I suggested to him that rather than going to lunch, he should go and knock on the door of three prospects that he knew might need his services. It was the last Friday of the month, and he dug deep within himself. He plucked up the courage, and enthusiasm, that it usually takes when things are a bit down. As a consequence, he made his best deal of the year. Just by knocking on one extra door!

Many would not have done that preferring to wait instead for that mythical, just right, moment that never arrives. As hard as it may seem the best time to make a sale is often just after you have suffered the disappointment of missing one.

That is the beauty of being in sales. As it turned out he still sold the car. When I enquired as to why he sold it, he told me that whilst he was dropping his eldest daughter to college on a beautiful summer's day some months later with the top down on the two-door Mercedes, he stopped at a pedestrian crossing for two schoolboys to cross. He overheard one pupil say to the other, "Did you see that dirty old man with that young girl in his flash car?" He sold it that same afternoon.

Whenever I'm feeling down, a bit rejected, or sorry for myself, I think of the late, dearly loved Dr Norman Vincent Peale. He always said that the only person without problems is in a graveyard. He would then ask the good Lord 'to please send him a mighty big problem'. He felt that the people who are most alive are the people with the biggest problems.

What habits must Pat improve, to go from mediocre to champion?

In Pat's case he has had a number of lean months as salespeople do. Despite claiming he was earning big money, his expenditure on a fancy lifestyle, a high maintenance partner, a rental suburban beachfront apartment certainly exceeded his income. He could not afford the fuel to get out there because he had exceeded his credit card limit, and had nothing left in his deposit account.

He was desperate for any commission, and as a result he had a huge big "I want your money" sign written all over his face. The client can always sense desperation. As a salesperson if you are desperate for

244

dollars then take action to ease the financial pain. Please, do yourself a favour and quietly get yourself a part-time job at night stacking supermarket shelves or something so that you are not so desperate.

Let me repeat, the client always senses desperation and will therefore, either not buy or be very hard to convince. Once you have to convince people, then they are not buying and you are not selling you are pressuring.

Chapter 45. **<u>Motivation From Within:</u>** Often takes an outsider to draw out.

We salespeople can sometimes be a handful. It goes with the territory. Internal managers can inspire us, but that can present challenges. Either the manager stays aloof all of the time, in which case we think they are rudely withdrawn or they become too friendly and over familiar with the team by regularly heading out on the town with them.

Once they do that they are exposed as being human and just like us. Then, even if they are the one who pays the wages, they are no longer as dramatic or taken quite as seriously. Familiarity can even generate some contempt, and that is why great sporting coaches remain professionally aloof from their team. They almost have to be introverted and extroverted in the same breath, so remain out of the team's social circle. A knockout master motivator usually comes through an external source and is from outside of the company.

This is where a colleague of mine John Gill comes into play. John has won nine world martial arts championships, and is the current world self-defence champion at age 49. John covers attitude in a very new, powerful and highly effective way. Many who have seen him in action say that he is a world class attitudinal package all bundled into one.

Talk about the X-Factor! To win his titles each year he has had to travel to the USA, and then prove that he is better at his craft than all the other international martial art experts are. He is living proof that 'Eagles don't hunt flies.' Consider a few of the attitudinal strengths that he needs to possess, and have deeply ingrained within to be able to use, often all in the same instant. These strengths would include loads of self-confidence, self-discipline, and self-belief. Then he must be able to have total focus on the task, no fear of rejection, no doubting himself. Add to that list; no last minute jitters.

He must also have the ability to put all of his endless hours of training into action in the blink of an eye. Enthusiasm - he has bucket loads of enthusiasm. The first impression you get of him is his passion for life; I love watching people who are passionate about their trade. "Action speaks louder than words," and "fear not, fire up" are his mantras. When his passion for selling and his enthusiasm for life, are combined, it is a dynamic mix.

It would take a very talented Hollywood actor to play the role of John Gill in a movie of his life, because this type of passion is hard to fake. It shows in his whole persona, in his eyes; you can pick it in his voice and his movements. People who attend his program are mesmerized and love watching and listening to his irresistible style. After this dynamic, empowering event, participants are energized, determined, and galvanised to take positive action. He lights an inspirational fire in their belly. John will give anyone and any team the attitudinal X-Factor.

This attitude beats any product knowledge expert. Prospects love buying from someone who is passionate and enthusiastic. This silently tells the prospect that the salesperson loves their job and, therefore, must believe deeply in their own product. A separate product specialist can be bought in to the sales cog specifically when required. John has a distinctive way of using his martial arts talents and disciplines.

He quickly transfers his passion to others, and if you need a team fired up he is the go to man. He injects excitement and enthusiasm into salespeople. He does so in such a unique way they will then do what is needed to sustain them at peak performance. He is one of those infectious, no limit, people who live their life to make a difference for the betterment of others.

John is a strong, honest member of the community and he has been three times nominated as Australian of the Year. Just a few months ago, I met up with him in Mt Gambier. He had driven about 100 kilometres to get there from one direction, and I had driven about 500 kilometres to get there from the other direction.

When I arrived, John was just farewelling a hitchhiker who he had picked up on the journey. To me, this hitchhiker looked like he may have been in Charles Manson's mob and I enquired about the mysterious man. John told me that he had seen him hitching on the side of the road and had figured that he preferred to have him in his car than in another car.

His logic was that if he unexpectedly caused any trouble John could deal with that. He preferred that option to the hitchhiker being in another car with someone who could not deal with any problems that may have occurred.

It transpired that the hitchhiker was a genuinely friendly bloke who had lived and worked in the area for many years, and his tales gave John a marvellous insight into the neighbourhood. That just shows how he thinks and how dependable the man is. Imagine if your entire team had that self-confidence. Not overconfidence, which sometimes leads to trouble. Rather, positive, healthy assertiveness that allows salespeople to overcome any obstacles, any adversity, and any rejection they may encounter to get to where they need to be.

John also runs anti-bullying programs for kids and self-defence for women throughout the country in his own time and at his own expense. He just loathes any form of violence, especially against women and children. All he asks in return is that the participants, if they are happy with him, simply donate to the White Ribbon Foundation, which is a charitable organisation that opposes violence against women.

Over the years, John has spent hundreds of thousands of dollars learning and perfecting his techniques to attain and keep his world champion status. He is a Sixth Dan Belt martial artist, and it fascinates me why he does it, but you only have to watch him for a few minutes and you can just see he is certainly passionate about what he does.

In the selling environment, attitude and enthusiasm are just priceless. It is surprising how quickly a good attitude session can positively affect people. A simple and immediate case that I've seen of such an attitude adjustment was when I was asked recently to talk to a member of a company. Their normal performance reviews did not have the desired effect. The manager felt that the person concerned was a tremendously valuable employee, but that employee often appeared to be depressed. She was worried because she had thought that because of this unhappiness he was going to leave and join an opposition company.

At the employer's invitation, I introduced myself to the employee, sat down for a while, and quietly asked him to list all the things that he liked about the company, and the people, that he was working with at that time. I borrowed a technique from Benjamin Franklin. I drew a line down the centre of a piece of blank paper and in the right-hand side made a column headed 'Yes.' I allowed time for the two of us, working together, to complete a list of all the benefits of staying with the company. We finished up with about 30 bullet points. Then, I asked him to complete the left hand side column headed 'No,' and handed it to him to fill out by himself.

I kept silent while he did that. On the left-hand side, he finished up with only 8 or 9 bullet points that the new company he was thinking of joining could offer him. We then compared each listing, and from that, he was able to tell me that the existing business was the better place to work. He stayed happily, without even so much as a new office, or a pay rise being offered. It is a powerful closing technique also known as "the Process of Elimination Close" where you re-cap on all the benefits. To answer the question whether or not you are in the right job, I guess each has to search into our own soul.

What habits must Pat improve, to go from mediocre to champion?

On the way home, Pat agreed to meet the next morning for a four-hour in-depth sales refresher session with me in my office. My office is away from his regular day-to-day office and, therefore, outside of his comfort zone. Pat also confirmed to me that the company sales trainers were exceedingly product orientated. When we had finished that four-hour session we broke everything down into the sales 'COG' segments, he slumped forward with his head in his hands. After some minutes, he looked up in anguish and said, "I seriously need to change my whole presentation approach, don't I?"

He agreed that he had, in fact, been shown many of the selling skills explained before but that he had just gradually forgotten how to apply them. Now to his credit, having now spent time with him over the last few months Pat has implemented a vast amount of material that we supplied him with and his coffers are swelling, as a result. Old habits die hard, so I have since given him a few refreshers. He said that the thing he likes the most about the refreshers is that it is coming from someone different; outside of the company and that, person does not know all of their foibles and weaknesses. Pat should consider new ways to:

- ❖ Have faith in his ability. If it is to be, it is up to me.

- ❖ Have faith in those around him.

- ❖ Take charge of his consequences.

- ❖ Keep reviewing and renewing the way he presents.

Chapter 46. **Referrals and Testimonials:** Your priceless allies.

It is always far more effective if the client hears about your skill and expertise from someone other than you. You can use basic things like well-written, well-presented genuine testimonials and case studies as proof of your credibility. Whilst many corporations are reluctant to allow their employees to endorse others' products, they will still provide a photo and a name. When asking for their testimonial, people often say to me, "Well Phil, you write it, and I will approve it and then you can put my name to it". Try to avoid this if you can because it is far more powerful and more credible if people use their own words. What they say about you may pleasantly surprise you and they will use words in a way that you have probably not thought of yourself.

Companies and corporations spend squillions of dollars on marketing and advertising their products and services. As their sales representative, their focus is on getting your foot in the door. Think about when you step into an unrelated business, once in the door you're left feeling frustrated because the people in the organisation do not necessarily give you a comfortable feeling, asking for directions is even difficult. Usually they will ignore you, and you feel as though you are interrupting their day if you ask them for something, such as for directions. To me everyone in the organisation should be a salesperson because you never know at which stage the client will pull out, possibly cancel their order or choose not to go ahead.

My bet is that cancelling is because someone has not closed properly, tied them down properly or given any decent service. Once people walk away from a place of business with the impression that they have been treated badly, then they tell about 20 people of their unsatisfactory experience. On the other hand, if they had been treated brilliantly, they will most likely tell only three or four people. Often those people will be the best friends and will tend to follow them in their buying decisions. Word of mouth is still the most powerful advertising.

Using COG, we always under promise and then burst our boilers to over deliver. Make sure everyone has been satisfied; the pleasurable experience means they will be happy to tell their friends. Ask them for those friends' names and they may give you five or six. At least three of those will be amongst the easiest sales you will ever make. Your satisfied client's original decision to buy from you has already done 90% of the sales effort for you. It is often, just the little things, which make all the difference.

Even, if your business is running well and you give yourself 100%. It is always far more effective if the client hears about your skill and expertise from someone other than you. You can use basic things like well-written, well-presented genuine testimonials as proof of your credibility. Whilst many corporations are reluctant to allow their employees to endorse others' products they will still provide a photo and a name.

Chapter 47. **Word Of Mouth:** Your most potent advocate.

Bad news travels but good news you have to carry. Your satisfied clients are the most compelling way to carry your good news. They will spread the word of mouth for you like a virus, so make sure it is good news they are carrying. People talk because it makes them feel good, they want to help others and they want to connect to people in their social group. Many live for it. One research specialist claims that mainly narcissistic people use Facebook, always trying to make their lives look interesting even if they are stuck at home tired and bored. They are people who have a consuming self-absorption or self-love; a type of egotism. Narcissists continually evaluate their appearance, desires, feelings, and abilities. They will try to make everything they do sound as exciting as they possibly can. Great, good for them, pamper to them. Go 'that little extra' to make them happy by treating them well and being kind to them.

Underselling, and over delivering, always beats over selling and under delivering, so keep your promises. Perhaps you are getting comments from unsatisfied clients; then do whatever you can think of to set matters right. Often a client or customer who feels aggrieved complains, receives great remedial service that fixes the problem, and that person who has then been satisfied, tells more people than someone who was satisfied right away. Odd isn't it?

You can use social media as a tool to speak directly with business, friends, and family, giving them a story to share. When people are talking about you, answer them. Budget your marketing effort carefully. You can use the abundance of websites on the Internet for a fraction of the cost and reach a far greater audience than traditional newspaper or magazines can give you. Let your satisfied clients do the talking for you with positive feedback about their experiences with you. Offer a 'friend-bring-a-friend' coupon and just keep spreading the word. To see how powerful the web is, Google the 'lip syncing kid' on YouTube. It is a fascinating story with millions of hits to a kid, who had been bullied at school, locked in his bedroom lip-syncing to his favourite tunes. The music artist, '50 Cent' heard about him and launched a song with the kid.

Use an email-delivery company that lets you track who forwards your newsletters - those are active talkers. Without a doubt, the most common thing many companies do is to give away email newsletters. They are easy to produce, relevant to the reader, and easy to pass along. Use something different, interesting, and memorable so that it helps increase the viral factor and people pass it along willingly. Create an online bulletin board or forum where past, present and prospective customers can talk to you and to each other.

Keep them on your website as long as you can because just like in a real live sales environment, once they leave they are not likely to come back. As the car, salespeople say, "There ain't no pity in be back city".

Chapter 48. **Success Stories:** "They did it my way!"

Selling for me is a marvellous occupation. It has made me many friends around the world, and I have received surprising accolades. In 1983, a lovely woman visited me; she was a few years younger than I was. She had been married, and her husband had been caught doing wrong at the finance company he worked for, and had left the job, the town, and her. To survive she had borrowed money off her elderly retired parents, and was desperate to repay them.

I advised her that the only way I knew how to do that would be to sell something and earn money. She asked if she could attend a few sales meetings with me and I agreed. At the time, one of our clients was a radio station. We were training their sales team. After a few sessions, they were so impressed with her enthusiasm that they employed her. Within three months, she had paid her parents back, and had a successful career in selling.

Some time ago, I met the CEO of a building company, the construction industry being the one I know and understand the best. He invited me to bring our team in to talk to his sales team and acknowledged that times were tough. When we subsequently presented our consulting fee to him, he told us immediately that he could not afford us.

We then replied that we would train his people in our professional, consultative sales methods provided his company paid us 2.5% of the profits generated by the increased sales we produced. After nine months of that he was begging us to get out of the arrangement because the 2.5% was just costing him way too much per month. Because it had worked well, and become so lucrative for us we hesitated at first. We later relented and he willingly agreed to go back to the original monthly consulting fee basis. In the mid 1990's, I was flying into Los Angeles and an elderly man stopped me and asked if I was Phil Polson. On replying, "Yes I am", his wife stepped forward and gave me a big hug and told me that she would not have been on this flight if it hadn't been for me. She explained that she had bought a set of Norman Vincent Peals audio tapes from me at a seminar some years earlier and those tapes had helped her address her fear of flying and this was their first trip away overseas.

The large brewery and hotel chain that we worked with over a number of years took our advice and implemented a system that we had recommended for handling any food, drink or service quality complaints that were received in any of their branded restaurants. The system meant that when any complaint was received, the next morning, the Area Restaurant Manager had to phone the complainant and personally apologise.

They had to set up a time to personally hand-deliver to the complainant's home an absolutely-free meal voucher, with a bonus wine bottle coupon, and hand them double their money back for the previous meal in cash at the same time. The idea actually had some interesting outcomes.

When one Area Manager followed up on an out of town couple who had complained that their restaurant experience had been an unpleasant one. Consequently, the Manager had to drive over five hours there and back through hilly countryside, much of it on class two winding roads, to deliver the gift to them. You can imagine the ripple effect that had down the line of command and through the organisation. The big three of food, drink, and service improved so much that complaints dropped to a negligible level within a short time and our contract was extended.

I conducted on-site consultancy and management training for several years on a major oil refinery, construction site. It was the second largest in the world at the time and the most sophisticated refinery ever built with 6,500 workers on site at peak. I flew in on a two weeks on, two weeks off schedule.

258

Repeating myself twice a day to different groups of twenty management people at a time ensured that the messages were always accurate, consistent and every issue was covered. There had been an accidental death prior to my starting. The first action that I recommended was to change the monster 4 metre high billboard from 'Negative, lost time statements' to a 'Positive Safety Awareness' message at the site entry.

With a graph of the safety campaign and time worked records highly visible. After five years the project was finished in under the internationally recognised 'Houston- gauge'. That gauge is a standard performance measurement for the heavy metal industry and showed we finished on time and on budget. The consortium of seven leading construction companies at a completion function presented me with a beautiful 'leather-bound' pictorial compendium, signed by all the 550 superintendents and supervisors, as a keepsake that is proudly displayed in my office to this day.

Another top sales performer who I thoroughly enjoyed working with was a man by the name of Charlie "Tremendous" Jones. Charlie is your quintessential brash loud American. He is about six foot five inches and is built like a brick outhouse. Charlie had been in sales since he was 16 years of age. He made his way to the top of the mutual funds industry in the USA until he retired and went on the speaking circuit. It is serious fun to be around him. When asked why his middle name is 'Tremendous', he will reply that whenever people ask him "How are you going Charlie?" he replies "tremendous" and it just stuck.

We invited him out to Australia and New Zealand. When he greeted me, having just arrived off the plane, he gave me a giant bear hug. While hugging he whispered in my ear "Whatever you do don't hug me back because everybody's watching, and they are all worried about us!" On then enquiring about his beloved wife's health, Charlie replied with a massive grin, jokingly saying, "Well she will not be happy because she knows the plane has landed safely, so she won't be able to cash in on my life insurance just yet". His central point when talking to sales and business audiences around the world was "If you think it is tough to make a dollar in selling now, then just wait to see how tough the future will be."

In 1997, I was conducting a sales training assignment for a substantial international telephone company and they had one particular salesperson there who was undoubtedly a person of considerable potential but had not had many sales successes in his time with them. They had not been able to get the best out of him.

The company invited me to spend time with him personally out in the field and also in his office helping them to write proposals. I accompanied him to a potential client, which was a well-established engineering company needing a large, highly technical telephone system. The clients were in the process of completing a brand new purpose-built building. They were looking for the right telephone solution.

I went through the same consultative sales process exactly as I have detailed in this book. The salesperson's technical skills were excellent and he picked up the sales skills remarkably quickly. He later attributed his success on this particular project to me because at last someone who knew what they were doing had taken the time to sit down with him and finesse his sales skills. The client was a substantial one by International standards and it was a perfect day when together we closed the deal and collected the initial investment payment. The client chose the financial option, which proved to be lucrative for both his company and himself.

Eighteen months later, he received a phone call from the chief executive of his company's biggest competitor. They invited him in for a meeting where they disclosed to him that they were certain that they had done enough at the time to win the engineering account. They further disclosed that while they were disappointed they had missed it, the client had said to them the reason they bought off my guy was that he had provided them with exactly the telephone solution they needed.

The CEO made him an offer to jump ship and join their company, he did. With his new and much enhanced retainer, plus healthy commission package, he was then able to borrow from the bank and purchase his first investment property from a client company of mine. Now, a decade and a half later, he has built such a strong property portfolio that he has retired at age 61 and lives comfortably off his rental income. We became firm friends and he has invited me to his wedding later this year.

Although my specialty is sales systems, working in the field is the only way I know to polish sales skills. I do it as often as possible. In 2000, after having driven nearly an hour to get to a prospective clients home I pulled up outside a well presented cottage with a white picket fence. As I was pulling up outside, a snowy haired gentleman in his late 50's came out of the gate. I was still getting out of the car and before I could introduce myself he told me that he was terribly sorry but he and his wife didn't want to waste my time that night because there was no way they could invest in anything. He indicated they had no spare money and were both close to retirement.

This presented a formidable challenge for me. I love them! I told him what I was doing there, and mentioned that as I had driven quite a way that it would be good to get out and stretch my legs. I also told him that the fact they thought they could not invest in anything was surely the very reason why they should spare some time with me. Their only cost for that would be a cup of tea and a biscuit. He agreed to that and took me inside to meet his lovely wife.

They had one grown-up son still living at home who was at university. We got chatting and it transpired that they were both in education. He was a school principal and she was an administrator at another school. They had spent their earnings sending all their children to private schools and to the best universities, and half jokingly said that they would be relying on their kids to feed them in their old age. My feelings are that all families' kids will have enough trouble trying to house and feed themselves, and their own children, to worry about housing and feeding good old Mum and Dad in their old age.

After about half an hour or so they gradually realised that with some help they could invest in a rental property. It would mean a little short-term sacrifice but within five years, it would be paying itself off. As a result of my meeting, with this couple that evening, the first property organised for them was a brand-new four-bedroom home at $110,000. Eleven years after, that property was valued at over $425,000. They now have two of them and are happily retired. Their superannuation and two lots of rent provide them with ample funds to live off. Plus, they have about $600,000 more in assets than they would've had if they hadn't spent the time to make a cup of tea for me 11 years ago. To this day, there are a number of their school teaching friends who remain as clients.

Probably the toughest assignment I have had in my sales training career, and the one I am most proud of, was an accountant who over the last few years has asked for my help. He is a lovely guy with a double degree in mathematics. He specialises at a level that is in the stratosphere compared to others. I have met quite a number of his clients.

Without exception, all have said how much he has contributed to their wealth and success. He has what every salesperson dreams of; a position of definite authority and credibility. However, like many professional people he has always felt the sales process to be a bit beneath him and therefore he has always taken the somewhat arrogant approach that he didn't need any sales systems. This accountant had mistakenly believed that you just get out there and tell enough people what you do, and as a result they will beat a path to your door.

Things changed considerably for him about five years ago, when his marriage collapsed. Later, as a result of that stress, he became ill. After that, some of the partners in the partnership that he was involved in decided to go their own separate ways. He took a payout which included a contract stating that he could not do work for his clients from the former partnership any more.

He found himself having to pay the two properties and having to pay for a new office with no clients. We got talking and over the last five years he has discovered within himself just how valuable he is, and now charges out of at around $800-$1,000 an hour. He continues to regularly up-skill himself by attending seminars on a wide a range of subjects that are of interest to himself and his clients. He has also been invited onto the board of a number of companies. He has learned to 'sell himself' and is now reaping substantial rewards for both himself and his client's. I hope one day soon to be able to add Pat to this list. Have I had failures? Of course I have, you can't learn unless you make a few mistakes, that is what life's about.

"Victory is sweetest, when you have known defeat."
Malcolm S. Forbes.

No doubt I have unintentionally made a few enemies along the way. This was never my intention, and frankly, after having done my best to try to resolve any issue, if it has not worked, I no longer have the spare time to dwell on that. I figure I can not do any better than my best.

My primary focus is on helping to make my clients wealthier, that is enriching for me. The purpose of this book is to show you how important salespeople and sales skill are. It provides powerful, indispensable sales skills and sales systems, which will help you to identify some areas and techniques to enhance your own selling ability. You can then make heaps more money and as a result enrich your life and those around you. I hope that you will then tell others about this book, and I can make some more money, as well. A win-win-win. You win, they win, and I win, "Fair enough?" He said with a smile. Have fun and good selling!

Some salespeople sit around waiting for the right psychological moment to make a sales call. Well congratulations you have just arrived at that precise moment. Selling takes courage, but often the things that take the most courage bring the biggest rewards. Now, what are you waiting for? Make it your best year ever.

Get out there and sell something!

Postface:

Large Events and Seminars organised and promoted by Phil Polson has included:

Speaker:	Subject:
Earl Nightingale	The Strangest Secret
Dr. Joseph Braysich	Body Language
E. James Rohn	Five Major Pieces to the Life Puzzle
Hal Krause	Planning Your Way to Financial Independence
Bobbie Gee	The Making of an Image
Roger Dawson	The Secrets of Power Negotiating.
Dr Charles Garfield	Achieving Peak Performance
Dr Robert Kreigel	The C Zone-Peak. Performance Under Pressure
Peter Johnson	The Designing of Sales Strategies.
Zig Ziglar	See You at the Top
Zig Ziglar	Secrets of Closing the Sale
Robert Johnson	Sell without Working
Charlie 'Tremendous' Jones	The Leading Edge for Sales
Dr Denis Waitley	The Winners Edge
Dr Denis Waitley	The Psychology of Winning
Dr Denis Waitley	Access 2000
Dr Norman Vincent Peale	The Power of Positive Thinking

Shannon Barnett	Communication, the Reality
Ed Foreman	Making Your Life More Terrific
Dr Robert Waterman	In Search of Excellence
Cavett Robert	Success with People
Amanda Gore	Managing Yourself and Your Life
Allan Pease	Body Language
Paul Dunn	Write right.
Peter H Thomas	Windows of Opportunity
Dr John Gray*	Men are From Mars, Women are From Venus
Dr Wayne Dyer*	How to Be the Best You Can Be
Louise L. Hay*	Heal Your Life
Deepak Chopra*	The Seven Spiritual Laws of Success
Joe Byrnes	Sales Motivation
Brad and Allan Antin	Skyrocket Your Sales
Brad and Allan Antin	Mastermind Your Business.

*In association with others.

Glossary of terms:

Benefits: descriptions of advantages, or profit, to be gained from owning your product or service. The term is often coupled with features. e.g. 'Features and benefits.'

Business model: defines the rationale, and the strategy in how the business will operate, by what means and to what end. There will be economic considerations as well as social, legal and other.

Buyer's remorse: a sense of regret that follows a purchase, the feeling that there was a better decision that could have been made. Buyer's remorse may be stronger as the size of the financial outlay increases.

Buy-line: an imaginary line that once the prospect steps over then they become buyers and you are no longer selling.

Closing: the tough stage at the end, the careful last communications that seal the deal.

Consultative Selling: a consultative sales approach is one that is not pushy, is ethical, shows professional competence and solves the needs of the client. This is an area where customers seek advice from the salesperson about the best steps forward.

Comfort Zone: a place, or situation where one feels safe, comfortable or at ease, and without stress. This is a realm where a person is comfortable and confident in, it may prove difficult to venture outside this. The zone may be determined by where their past success has been.

Commission: a performance based payment. This may be a set percentage of the sales price, or a set amount per item sold.

Cold Calling: making the initial communication with potential clients by either phoning them or knocking on their door without their prior knowledge or consent. Cold calling legislation applies in a lot of countries. Their address and phone number and details will likely come from a database.

Closing ratio: the ratio of qualified leads presented to compared to actual sales closed.

Conditions: differ from objections in that they no possible answer that can over come them.

Cooling off period: a set period of time either governed by law, or extended with negotiation in which the contractee can rescind the agreement.

Discovery schedule: the process of identifying personal, or business, needs and determining solutions to those problems. The person who carries out this task is an analyst.

Database: an organised collection of data that is referenced for information, this is an essential tool in listing potential prospects, tracking existing customers and generally maintaining large amounts of information..

Features: the distinctive attributes or aspects of your product, or service. The term is coupled with benefits. e.g. 'Features and benefits.'

Habits: be aware of both your own habits and your client's habits. Habits are a settled or regular tendency or practice, especially one that is hard to give up. Could lead to an addictive practice. Making a habit of using all the steps in the Sales Cog will ensure you sell more.

Intensifying the need: a technique in sales that involves drawing attention to, and/or attaching a great magnitude to how important the need that a customer has for the product or service that is being sold.

Incentive program: a promise that with a certain performance target reached, either across a sales team or tailored to an individual, a reward will be given on top of usual earnings.

Houston Gauge: an oil refinery was constructed in Houston Texas in the 1960's under perfect conditions. The weather was fine, skilled staff were available for immediate employment and all materials were close by. An allowance has been taken into account for various advents that have since occurred, which might lead to a deceleration of physical labour performance. Factors such as the advent of the potato chip, colour television, computers etc. Refineries build since have been measured by that gauge of performance.

Lead: obtaining the contact details of potential clients; a lead may be obtained in response to advertisement, from a referral, or from your own initiatives.

Lead generating: the proactive stage in collecting leads.

Netiquette: Internet, or network etiquette, it is a set of rules that prescribe refinements to communication via technology. E.g., e-mails should not be written all in uppercase; this would be read as if you were yelling at the respondent.

Neurolinguistic programming (NLP): explores the relationships between how we think (neuro), how we communicate (linguistic) and our patterns of behaviour and emotion (programmes).

Objections: elements of resistance to a product or service, and something that a prospect should be guided through carefully.

Pareto principle: also known as the 80-20 rule, which states that, for many events, roughly 80% of the effects come from 20% of the causes. In business maybe 80% of total sales come from 20% of the clients.

Photo chromatic glass: the glass wall turns dark, effectively becomes a closed curtain, when the light inside it is turned on and returns to its normal, see through transparency when the light is turned off.

Presentation: This is the sales pitch, from meeting a potential client to guiding them to a close. There are many aspects to be planned and refined.

Prospect: a potential buyer/user of your product/service.

Prospecting: the search to find buyers that fit the criteria you have outlined as the ideal customer/client, in property one aspect of the criteria is the potential buyers borrowing capacity.

Proposal: the offer stage, it may be verbal or written (or both) and is the stage where you and the client decide on what both parties obligations will be in the exchange.

Proxemics: the study of the cultural, behavioural, and sociological aspects of spatial distances between individuals.

Qualifying: an analysis of how the potential prospect fits the relevant factors in the profile of clients who most likely need or want the solution that you offer. e.g. qualify by age, salary, location, gender, occupation, net worth, asset base.

Referrals: when a satisfied client or customer recommends your product or service to a third party, usually by word of mouth or letter of introduction.

Relationship Manager: a person responsible for managing a company's interactions with customers, clients and sales prospects.

Return on Investment. (ROI): the amount of money returned over and above that spent on products and services that offer to create wealth or profits. The customer will be interested in how much money their investment in this product or service will return.

Salespeople: the driving force behind making a sale; they come in many shapes and sizes and should be valued for, and played, to their strengths.

Sales audit: a review of the methods, tools, and people involved in selling by a prospect, it should be objective.

Sales flu: borrowed from 'flu' (Influenza). When sales results, or salespeople are not in good shape.

Spam: the use of an electronic medium to send bulk amounts of messages indiscriminately. The usual understanding of spam is in the form of email advertisements.

Technical jargon: the area of discussion in which the finer details of a product are observed, it is also the industry specific language in which to discuss these.

Testimonials: when a customer makes a written or verbal statement about your product or service to another, this is a useful tool in backing up the claims you make to a prospective buyer.

The Disturb: taking someone out of their comfort zone, selling technique in which the salesperson creates a fear within the prospect that if they don't change their current situation (i.e. by buying the product on offer) they will be somehow disadvantaged.

Tying Down: getting confirmation from the prospect that they agree with what you have just proposed or covered, formalising the discussion, into a concluded sale. This may involve the signing of a contractual agreement.

Webinar: a web based seminar, keeping up with the technological age and allowing access for people in a broad geographical area. Cost effective, and can be attended from ones own home or office.

X-Factor: The French say a special 'je ne sais quoi'. Something that you might not be able to put your finger on, but this is the element that makes you the salesperson, your presentation, or the product appeal that much more to the prospect.

ABOUT THE AUTHOR

Roger Dawson is widely acknowledged as an expert in the art of negotiating and is a full-time professional speaker on the subjects of Power Negotiation, Power Persuasion and Confident Decision Making. He is the author of *Secrets of Power Negotiating*, one of the largest selling business cassette programmes ever published. The National Speakers Association has awarded him the CPAE, its highest honour for public speaking

A nice endorsement from Roger Dawson.

Playing 'Bridge' on the Island Princess

Paul Marston taught me to play some Bridge. He accompanied us on the Island Princess Seminars as the Bridge Instructor. Paul founded the Grand Slam Bridge Club, in Double Bay, NSW, Australia. He is widely regarded as one of the worlds leading authorities on the game of Bridge. Add to that his selection to represent both New Zealand and Australia at the card game he loves. He has written numerous best-selling books on the subject and has a regular newspaper column.

The article appeared in the Financial Review. Feb 13th 1987.

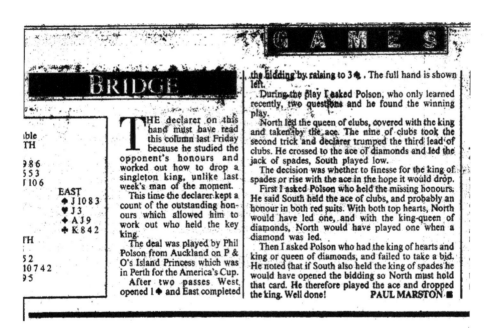

GAMES

BRIDGE

THE declarer on this hand must have read this column last Friday because he studied the opponent's honours and worked out how to drop a singleton king, unlike last week's man of the moment.

This time the declarer kept a count of the outstanding honours which allowed him to work out who held the key king.

The deal was played by Phil Polson from Auckland on P & O's Island Princess which was in Perth for the America's Cup.

After two passes West opened 1♦ and East completed the bidding by raising to 3♣. The full hand is shown left.

During the play I asked Polson, who only learned recently, two questions and he found the winning play.

North led the queen of clubs, covered with the king and taken by the ace. The nine of clubs took the second trick and declarer trumped the third lead of clubs. He crossed to the ace of diamonds and led the jack of spades, South played low.

The decision was whether to finesse for the king of spades or rise with the ace in the hope it would drop.

First I asked Polson who held the missing honours. He said South held the ace of clubs, and probably an honour in both red suits. With both top hearts, North would have led one, and with the king-queen of diamonds, North would have played one when a diamond was led.

Then I asked Polson who had the king of hearts and king or queen of diamonds, and failed to take a bid. He noted that if South also held the king of spades he would have opened the bidding so North must hold that card. He therefore played the ace and dropped the king. Well done!   PAUL MARSTON ■

EAST
♠ J 10 8 3
♥ J 3
♦ A J 9
♣ K 8 4 2

A major oil refinery construction site.

Part of the leather bound keepsake presentation given to me at the completion of the Marsden Refinery Project in which I conducted Management consulting for the projects approximately 550-600 construction Supervisors and Foremen. Under the title 'Management Awareness Programme 'MAP'. The massive project was completed on time and on budget. We finished under the 'Houston Gauge', which is an internationally recognised performance measurement for the heavy metal construction industry. The manual that was written during the project still forms the basis of most heavy metal manuals to this day. Talk about standing out like a sore thumb, I was the only guy in a suit on the project.

The gentleman depicted as patting me is Bill Raymond, a leading Canadian Engineer. He was a pleasure to work with. That's me in the left centre proclaiming to have 'taught them all they know'. Bill is saying 'keep taking your tablets Phil you'll be OK. This was a light-hearted dig at my habit of taking daily vitamin tablets. In the evening a lot of us played golf at the local course. Talk about a team of champions. I cut the moustache off long after the cartoon was given to me.

INDEX

Index

Index

ISBN 978-1468032086

Printed in Great Britain
by Amazon.co.uk, Ltd.,
Marston Gate.